Computer-to-Plate Primer

by Richard M. Adams and Frank J. Romano

GATFPress
Pittsburgh

Copyright 1999
Graphic Arts Technical Foundation
All Rights Reserved

International Standard Book Number: 0-88362-236-X
Library of Congress Catalog Card Number: 99-64455

Printed in the United States of America
GATF Catalog No. 1598

Reproduction in any form by any means without specific written permission is prohibited.

Individual trademarks are the property of their respective owners. Product names are mentioned in this book as a matter of information only and do not imply endorsement by the Graphic Arts Technical Foundation.

Printed on 70-lb. Monadnock Astrolite Smooth.

GATF*Press* books are widely used by companies, associations, and schools for training, marketing, and resale. Quantity discounts are available by contacting Peter Oresick at 800/910-GATF.

GATFPress	**Orders to:**
Graphic Arts Technical Foundation	GATF Orders
200 Deer Run Road	P.O. Box 1020
Sewickley, PA 15143-2600	Sewickley, PA 15143-1020
Phone: 412/741-6860	Phone (U.S. and Canada): 800/662-3916
Fax: 412/741-2311	Phone (all other countries): 412/741-5733
Email: info@gatf.org	Fax: 412/741-0609
Internet: http://www.gatf.org	Email: gatforders@abdintl.com

TABLE OF CONTENTS

Foreword v

Timeline vii

1 **Introduction to CTP** 1

2 **Job Engineering** 11

3 **Raster Image Processing** 27

4 **Proofing** 45

5 **The Image Carrier** 57

6 **Quality Control** 71

7 **Workflow** 87

8 **Return on Investment** 93

Glossary 99

About the Authors 113

About GATF 115

GATFPress: Selected Titles 117

FOREWORD

A crash course in computer-to-plate technology? Yes, that's what we have asked of Richard M. Adams, research scientist/digital imaging and color reproduction specialist at GATF, and Frank J. Romano, professor of graphic arts at Rochester Institute of Technology. This book offers a short, non-technical orientation to the field.

The aim of the GATF*Press* primer series is to communicate the essential concepts of printing processes and technologies. Other primers focus on lithography, flexography, gravure, on-demand, digital, and screen printing, and new titles are being planned.

Computer-to-Plate Primer is useful to students, graphic artists, print buyers, publishers, salespeople in the graphic communications industry—to anyone who would like to know more about the printing process.

GATF*Press* is committed to serving the graphic communications community as a leading publisher of technical information. Please visit the GATF website at http://www.gatf.org for additional information about our resources and services.

Peter Oresick
Director
GATF*Press*

CTP TIMELINE

- 1974: The first computer-to-plate (CTP) system was the Lasergraph. It used two high-powered lasers to burn off nonrelief areas of a solid block of plastic to produce a letterpress plate. It almost printed a newspaper in Elmira, New York.

- 1976: An EOCOM CTP system was demonstrated at the ANPA newspaper show in Anaheim, California. A test installation was installed in a Utica, New York, newspaper.

- 1985: Computer-to-plate technology was applied for the *Wall Street Journal, New York Times,* and *Christian Science Monitor.* A pasteup of the pages was scanned to produce the data for exposing plates. The *Journal* and *Monitor* used satellites to send pages across the United States. The *Times* sent them across the river to New Jersey.

- 1986: The IBM/Hell/EOCOM/Autologic CTP system was installed at the Morristown, New Jersey, *Daily Record.* The EOCOM flatbed platesetter was demonstrated in 1984 and later sold to Gerber. It was part of the Autologic APPS-1 system, which was the first system to assemble a newspaper digitally and expose the plate from that data. It was installed briefly in Morristown on its way to obscurity.

- 1990: Polyester plates were introduced in the mid-1980s and exposed in early versions of photographic imagesetters. In 1990 Hoechst (Kalle) presented the N90 CTP plate at DRUPA, a major international printing equipment exhibition held every five years. In 1990 almost all printing plates were exposed in vacuum frames.

- 1991: Presstek and Heidelberg introduced the first on-press platemaking system with the Heidelberg GTO-DI. The system is now used for two-up and four-up presses as well as off-line platemaking for wet or dry plates. A Gerber LE55 (EOCOM) was installed at a Netherlands newspaper and exposed the N90 plate.

- 1994: The first publication produced completely computer-to-plate was *Sports Car International* in May. Publisher's Press in Florence, Kentucky, used an Optronics Platesetter for the glossy four-color edition. Publisher's Press now uses Gerber platesetters and scans ad films to produce digital files.

- 1995: The first publication with advertising supplied digitally and produced computer-to-plate was *The Computer in the 21st Century* from Scientific American, published in April. Apple Computer was the only advertiser and its agency, BBDO, supplied digital ads for printer R.R. Donnelley's Creo platesetters. In May there were more CTP systems installed at DRUPA (42) than in user plants around the world.

- 1997: More CTP systems were installed than in all other years combined.

- 1998: As of December, there were 3,090 aluminum-based offset CTP systems worldwide.

- 1999: There are now more than 30 digital plates and over 57 models of CTP platemakers.

1 Introduction to CTP

The four-color, 84-page May 1994 issue of *Sports Car International* has claimed a unique place in the history of printing. It was the first glossy four-color magazine in the world printed on a web offset press from plates imaged entirely without film; not a single plate was made from photographic film.

The technology that permitted this is computer-to-plate technology. CTP, or direct-to-plate as it is sometimes called, is a digitized plate-imaging process. Publishers provide all editorial and advertising content in digital form (either on disk or by sending the data over telephone lines) to printers who, in turn, electronically produce printing plates, eliminating all the traditional intermediate film-preparation stages.

Anyone who has been reading the trade press over the past few years or has attended trade exhibitions is aware of the enormous interest in CTP. What began in the late 1980s and early 1990s as a trickle has become a river. There are more than 57 CTP system models sold by 24+ firms with about 30+ plates. Some systems expose a variety of plates; some concentrate on one plate.

The trend in printing is toward shorter run lengths, which means changing plates more often. CTP seems to be the primary method for conventional lithography to cope with the continuously growing demand for short-run printing and increased productivity. Potentially, investing in CTP can provide the following benefits:

- A reduction in the amount of supplies—such as film, carrier sheets, film chemicals, tapes, and adhesives—that need to be purchased.
- A reduction in the number of personnel needed, specifically

in the areas of stripping, film/plate exposure, retouching, and processing.
- A reduction in prepress costs by the elimination of various equipment, such as that used in film/plate exposure, film processing, and maintenance.
- An increase in floor space of up to 50%.
- A savings in production time (from digital file to plates).
- Improved workflow due to a more streamlined operation.
- Improved quality due to greater predictability in using first-generation digital data.

A major drawback, however, is the cost of entry. CTP means more than installing a plate imaging device. A CTP installation involves many additional devices and systems that enable the application of a digital workflow. New organizational and technological requirements are created (networking, storage and archiving, digital proofing, file transfer, preflighting). Equipment such as the platesetter, peripherals, and digital proofing equipment must be purchased; a digital infrastructure created; high-speed networks and mass storage systems put in place; and systems integration and training provided. All must be implemented for the switch to computer to plate.

You can quickly categorize the systems into two-up (i.e., printing two pages on the same sheet using the same plate), four-up, and eight or more-up, although some systems can handle both four-up and eight-up. Then you can categorize them by dry or wet processing. The wet processing can be water for the photopolymer plates or chemistry for the silver-based plates. Some of the dry processing requires a smidgen of water.

There are three types of computer-to-plate systems currently in use:
- Plates or image carriers for gravure and flexography on which the images can be produced by etching with high-powered lasers or electromechanical engraving devices.

- High-speed light-sensitive plates for lithography with coatings that have light sensitivities on the order of litho film and that can be exposed with low-power visible lasers.
- Non-light-sensitive plates for lithography with coatings on which images can be produced by heat (infrared) radiation rather than light.

SYSTEM SETUP

The automated nature of CTP technology lends itself to flexible placement of the system. There is some debate as to whether the platesetter should be installed in the prepress area, the plateroom, or the pressroom.

Each location has advantages and disadvantages in the great scheme of digital workflow. To place the platesetter in the pressroom is the most problematic area since dust, vibration, and environmental conditions may adversely affect the system. At present, some of the Creo systems are designed for placement in the press area, and are sealed and conditioned for such areas. However, the vast majority of CTP users have chosen to install the platesetter in the area formerly used for traditional platemaking, or an area adjacent to it. A few users have placed the platesetter in an area where imagesetters are also installed.

A large-format platesetter will typically measure six or more feet square, and weigh up to 1 ton or more. As well as the space taken up by the processing line itself, the surrounding area must be free for access and work activities. The positioning will therefore require either the provision of a separate room, or have space made available for it on the pressroom floor.

COMPONENTS

Components of a computer-to-plate system include a raster image processor, or RIP; a plate-holding area; systems for slip sheet removal, punching, and loading and unloading plates; a platesetter; and a post-processing system.

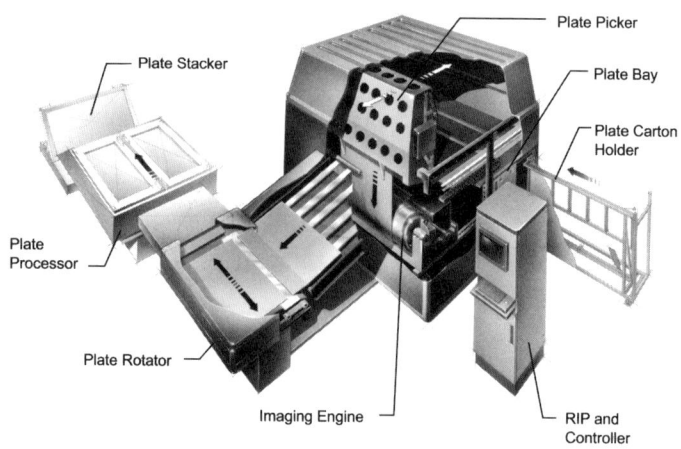

A look inside the Creo Platesetter 3244.

Digital Front End or Raster Image Processor

The DFE, or RIP, prepares a screened bilevel bitmap for each color separation, which drives the imaging system to image each plate.

Unimaged Plate-Holding Area

Plates are stored in a light-tight loading area, usually in special cassettes; although, some plate suppliers will offer packaging that does not require re-handling of plates. If the automatic plate-handling option is not selected, the platesetter must be installed in a darkroom if light-sensitive plates are used. New thermal plates require yellow light conditions or may operate in daylight.

Slip Sheet Removal

Automatic systems must deal with slip sheets. All of them have developed approaches that sense the difference between the slip sheet and the aluminum plate and thus can deal with the sheet and then select the plate. Automatic plate handling contributes to overall productivity. Plates supplied come with interleaving paper sheets between each plate.

PLATE-LOADING MECHANISM
A mechanical system must sense the interleaf sheet and remove it, then "grab" the plate and transport it to the plate-imaging area. Usually some sort of suction system is used.

PUNCHING MECHANISM
There is still debate over whether to punch the plate before or after exposure. It usually cannot be done in the imaging area because of the delicacy of the optics.

PLATE-IMAGING AREA
Your selection of a platesetter will depend upon the size of plates you want to expose using CTP, but generally speaking, the larger the format and the higher the resolution required, the more money it is going to cost. We can categorize systems as:
- 66×82 in. very large format
- 55×67 in. large format
- 41×52 in. format
- 32×42 in. format
- 22×28 in. format

Platesetter models are internal drum, external drum, and flatbed. The fundamental differences among platesetters are the plate-holding method and the exposure source.

Platesetter manufacturers, except basysPrint, use lasers as the imaging energy source. The wavelength and power determine what plates may be used, and especially how fast they may be imaged. The choice of internal, external, or flatbed platesetter affects both the plates and the applicable pin register systems that may be used. Drum plate-holding systems curve or bend the plates, which will affect pinning options. Drum designs require less floor space than flatbed designs, but optional plate-loading unit space requirements reduce the advantage if plate-handling automation is required. This latter capability results from the light sensitivity of most plates and the need for darkroom conditions. This does not include thermal plates, which are not light-sensitive.

Flatbed. Flatbed configurations offer the simplest handling of plates and pin registration systems. Imaging methods involve complex optics. A rotating mirror scans a laser beam across the width of a plate with the laser scan limited to less than 22 in. by optics considerations. A plate, on a flat platen, moves perpendicularly to the laser scan direction, one bit position per laser scan. Special lenses are used to compensate for the change in focus as the laser beam is scanned across the flat surface, limiting the resolution. Very-high-speed imaging is possible. Makers of flatbed systems use multiple imaging heads or mechanical scanning methods. The matching (stitching) of the adjacent exposure areas is difficult, and the naked eye can often see a distortion pattern caused by an error a micron or smaller in size.

Overall, for flatbeds:
- Plates are easier to handle.
- A single-beam laser is used, and in some systems is only a short distance from the plate.
- Spot distortion across the image area from the laser beam starts to become a problem with image sizes greater than 22 in.

Internal drum. An internal-drum configuration mounts the plate on the inside surface of a partial cylinder, usually open at one or both ends. Physical loading and unloading of the plates is complicated, especially in the accommodation of registration pin sets. The configuration provides a low number of moving parts, simple optics, and no drum run-up time before imaging can start. A spinning deflection mirror moves along the axis, one bit space per revolution. This mirror deflects the laser, perpendicular to the axis, to the plate on the internal surface of the cylinder. A focusing element on the rotating mirror assembly projects the collimated beam onto the surface of the plate at the desired spot size. As the beam is

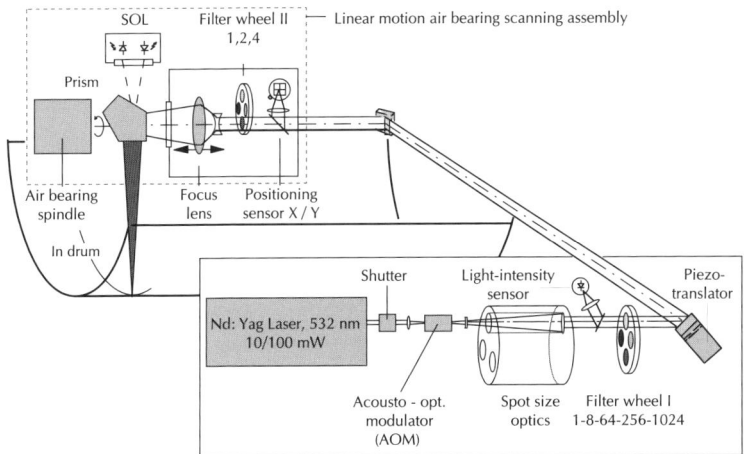

Internal drum platesetter from Heidelberg Prepress.

scanned around the partial circumference of the drum, the distance from the focusing lens to the plate surface is constant, and the beam stays in focus without complex optics. A bit stream from the RIP-produced bitmap modulates the laser beam. With each rotation, the beam images a track across the plate. The mirror assembly moves one bit position per revolution, so successive tracks are written one bit position apart. Harmonic vibration in the mirror assembly motion may cause "banding" on the plates as tracks are written close together, then far apart. All internal-drum designs use a single beam to expose the plate. The spinning mirror rotates at very high speed for high-speed imaging. Thus, the exposure spot dwells on a bit position for a very short time. The short imaging time per bit affects or is affected by the exposure characteristics of the plate. Ablative plates respond well to high-power, short-pulse exposure, but polymer materials respond better to a longer exposure pulse.

Overall for internal drums:
- Plate exposure is roughly the same size as the film it exposes.
- With single beam laser addressing, the plate bed remains static, keeping the plate firm.

	The Variations of Computer-to Technology
CTF	**Computer to Film** Raster-based imagesetters, both capstan- and drum-oriented.
CTIF	**Computer to Imposed Film** Imposetters, 4-up and larger format.
CTP	**Computer to Plate** Computer-to-plate, any kind of plate.
CTPP	**Computer to Polyester Plate** Imagesetters or imposetters, outputting film or plate, or dedicated devices that only output polyester plates.
CTAP	**Computer to Aluminum Plate** Platesetters using internal or external drum, flatbed, or curved approaches.
CTPoP	**Computer to Plate on Press** Presstek technology presently integrated on presses from Heidelberg and Omni-Adast.
CTPIC	**Computer to Plate Image Cylinder** Creo's developmental technology that involves spraying a material on a press cylinder and imaging it with thermal lasers.
CTEP	**Computer to Electronic Printer** Includes all digital printout devices, monochrome or color.
CTECP	**Computer to Electronic Color Press** Specifically involves high-end higher-speed color printing systems.

- The single laser beam works at only partial efficiency. To compensate for this, the mirror used rotates at 18,000 rpm.
- It is difficult to register to pins on an internal device.

External drum. An external-drum configuration mounts the plate on the outside of a rotating cylinder, almost like a plate being mounted on a press. Plate handling is complex as in all drum designs, and pin registration system configurations are limited. The laser beam(s) are perpendicular to the axis of the cylinder and focus on the surface of the plate. The optical path remains constant as the drum rotates. The exposure head moves on a track parallel to the cylinder axis. Multiple exposure beams can be used to speed imaging. There are a number of multiple beam interleaving methods. The laser head advances and each beam writes one of the tracks. Optronics, Presstek, and Barco Graphics systems apply a different method of interleaving multiple beams. The weight or mass of the plate limits the rotation speed of the drum. This low rotation speed allows the spot dwell time to be longer than an internal drum. The external-drum optics are simple, but slow rotation speed makes multiple beam designs essential for speeds that compete with internal drums and flatbeds.

Overall for external drums:
- The laser address source can be close to the plate.
- Because the imagesetters are used for both film and plates, there have been inherent physical problems with ensuring that the plate is secured to the drum. Film is normally secured by a pin system which is inappropriate for a plate, so various clamping methods are improvised.
- External drums are not efficient if addressed by a single laser beam, or else the drum has to be rotated at very fast speeds to accept the exposure, leading to potential problems with stability once the plate is loaded.
- Fast-spinning external drums potentially offer a hazard if the plate comes loose during imaging.

PLATES

The open questions are quality, consistency, and the lowest achievable price. Being very sensitive, early CTP plates had some problems in consistency, calling into question one of the most often mentioned benefits of CTP. Fewer steps in the production chain do not always guarantee consistency if those steps are not consistent. There are now several suppliers for CTP plates on the market, thus increasing competition and quality as well as regulating prices.

Plate-Unloading Mechanism

A mechanism releases the plate from the imaging area and transports it to an exit slot or to a conveyor connected to an on-line processor.

Post-Imaging Processing

All plates require some form of processing to either develop the image or at least wash away nonimage areas. To accomplish this, we can have the processor online or offline.

Some thermal plates require a pre-heating step after imaging but prior to processing, which essentially washes off the nonimage areas. Some thermal plates also require post-baking (after processing) to improve run length characteristics.

2 Job Engineering

The process of creating pages usually begins with a computer system equipped with word processing, illustration, scanning, and page layout software. These "front ends" (the "back end" being the imagesetter or platesetter) are usually Macintosh or PC/Windows microcomputers, but can also include UNIX-based systems.

Unless you already have digital prepress, going into CTP will mean additional investments, such as the purchase of computer workstations, data storage devices, a raster image processor (RIP), scanners, and other peripherals, including digital proofing devices. Software will also need to be purchased to perform a wide variety of functions, such as word processing, page layout, illustration, image editing, trapping, imposition, file checking, and calibration. In addition, networking and telecommunications capabilities also must be implemented.

SYSTEM REQUIREMENTS

In addition to the computer, or CPU, important components of the "front end" include memory, storage, removable media, and the display.

Memory

One important hardware consideration in any desktop publishing system is random-access memory (RAM), measured in megabytes (MB). RAM consists of circuit boards that provide workspace for the CPU. As operations are performed, the computer loads software commands and data, including text and images, from the hard disk into RAM. The operating system can execute commands and access data in RAM at a much higher speed than it can on the hard disk. However, RAM is volatile, meaning that items stored there will disappear when the power is shut off.

To run graphics applications efficiently, it is necessary to upgrade the computer with larger amounts of RAM. When working with image files, for example, fastest processing will be achieved when the software can access RAM that is three times greater than the largest image. With large upgrades, the RAM chips may cost more than the computer itself.

For image processing, the RAM requirements for your workstation will depend upon the volume of data required to be processed, but bear in mind the higher the resolution of the work carried out, the larger the amount of data.

Storage

In most cases, the operating system, software application programs, and documents created on the computer are stored on an internal magnetic storage device known as a hard disk. Hard disk capacity is usually specified in gigabytes (GB). Access time, the amount of time it takes to find a specified item on the hard disk, is specified in microseconds. With increasing capability, the capacity of hard disks has gone up, access time has improved, and cost has gone down. Typically, the least amount of hard disk space shipped today is 2 GB.

The larger the full-page file is, the more memory needed when running software applications. You will therefore have to carefully plan for intermediate storage of data, which will allow for continuous workflow if the system is not going to stop halfway through when it runs out of storage space. Although calculations will necessarily only be approximate when putting together the workstation equipment, a processing workstation should have:
- RISC (reduced instruction set computer) configuration if possible
- Clock speed of at least 300 MHz

- At least 128 MB of RAM, or possibly 256 MB
- Large hard disk with direct access (SCSI or USB)

REMOVABLE MEDIA

Only a few imposed sheets in RIPed form can be stored on a 500-MB hard disk before it runs out of space. The pixel content of a single 27.5×39.3-in. page at 2540 dpi in just one color adds up to an astounding 874 MB. In this case, one has to use hard disk arrays of at least 10-GB or, even better, 20-GB capacity. For processing high-quality color jobs, these arrays need to be 40 or 60 GB. Arrays with this sort of capacity can incorporate built-in fail-safe systems for sensitive data. Digital audio tape (DAT) can be used for archiving, having up to 8-GB storage volume, but DAT is relatively slow to access; although as a medium, it is considerably cheaper than hard disk.

In addition to the hard disk, it is necessary to have a method of transporting software and documents between computers. Removable media refers to a range of transportable storage media, including random-access disk drives and non-random-access tape drives. Random-access devices include magnetic, optical, and magneto-optical systems.

When examining the cost-effectiveness of storage media, it is helpful to calculate the cost per megabyte of media. This is done by dividing the cost of a disk or tape by the capacity.

GRAPHICS DISPLAYS

Computer displays can be classified according to size (inches, measured diagonally) and number of colors displayed (bit depth). The most efficient displays for desktop publishing are two-page displays that measure 19-, 20-, or 21-in. diagonally. Half-page, 17-in. displays are also popular. Smaller (13-, 14-, and 15-in.) displays are most commonly sold for home use.

Creation of black-and-white pages can be done on grayscale, or 8-bit, displays that can reproduce 256 gray levels. For creating color pages, 24-bit displays are most useful. These can specify 256 levels each of red, green, and blue (RGB), for a total of 16.7 million colors. When working with color monitors, it is important to remember that 24-bit circuitry can specify 16.7 million colors for display. The monitor's imaging system, however, may not be capable of reproducing this many colors, and studies have shown that the human eye is capable of seeing only about 10 million colors.

DIGITAL PHOTOGRAPHY

Digitization of pictures can be done through digital cameras and scanners. More features, higher quality, and lower cost have made digital cameras competitive with scanners for image capture, especially when quick turnaround is desired, as in computer-to-plate workflow. More service bureaus and printers are adopting digital photography as a way to recapture some of the high-end scanning revenue lost to the desktop systems in their clients' offices. There are currently more than 40 digital cameras on the market, and making the leap into the digital arena involves a lot of homework and planning.

Consumer cameras. The majority of digital cameras on the market are "consumer-based," ranging from several hundred to a few thousand dollars. They are often used by Internet developers who need quick shots to post on their sites. Other uses include real estate, police file imaging, and school newspapers. Although limitations in file size and compatibility with studio lighting often preclude their use in print production, image quality and file size are steadily increasing to the point where some consumer cameras can even compete with mid-range cameras.

Mid-range cameras. Priced from about $5,000 to $25,000, mid-range digital cameras differ greatly in function and capability. Most are stand-alone systems that give a higher quality image than consumer cameras, but with similar functions. These cameras can be used to capture images that require a fast turnaround time and that will be used in offset lithographic reproduction. The Associated Press uses digital cameras so its photographers can capture an image and within minutes download it to a remote laptop that can then send the image via modem and cell phone to a server for immediate retrieval.

High-end cameras. Priced from $25,000 to $55,000, the high-end digital cameras are usually used by photographers with a high volume of repetitive work. They are ideal for catalogs, circulars, and other applications where photos have the same set, lighting, viewing angle, and scene framing. Generally not stand-alone devices, they are used with medium-format or view cameras. Most systems in this range have a single charge-coupled device (CCD) sensor array with 2048×2048 pixels.

SCANNERS

Copy for scanning is divided into three modes, depending upon the number of colors and resultant computer space required. It is important to scan using the correct mode, as higher-color modes require more storage space and processing time. Modes can be converted from higher to lower (more colors to fewer colors), for example, from RGB color to grayscale or bitmapped modes.

Bitmapped images are represented with 1 bit of computer memory, yielding two colors: black and white. Bitmapped mode is used for scanning line art, including black-and-white logos and diagrams. This type of work, however, is preferably produced using a vector-graphic illustration program.

Grayscale images are represented with 8 bits of computer memory, which yields 256 (2^8) levels of gray. This mode is used for scanned halftones of black-and-white pictures.

Color images are represented with 8 bits each of red, green, and blue (RGB) color, totalling 24 bits or 16.7 million colors (2^{24}). Before printing, RGB color images must be converted to CMYK (cyan, magenta, yellow, and black) format, in which 8 bits are used to represent each color.

KINDS OF SCANNERS

Four basic scanner types may be distinguished. Desktop flatbed scanners are 8½×11 or 11×17-in. intended primarily for scanning line art and black-and-white or color prints. Options are sometimes available for scanning transparencies, but the scanner's resolution limits enlargement capability. Flatbed scanners use CCD light detectors with a dynamic range, or density range, of 3.3 or less. For color photos, conversion from RGB to CMYK color is done by the host computer.

Desktop slide scanners are intended for scanning transparencies only, including positive (slides) and negative (black-and-white and color negative film). Various models scan 35-mm only, or 35-mm, medium-format (2¼×2¼-in.), and 4×5-in. transparencies. As with desktop flatbed scanners, CCD light detectors are used, dynamic range is up to 3.3, and the host computer performs RGB-to-CMYK conversion.

Desktop drum scanners represent a trend toward bringing the quality of high-end drum scanning to the desktop. Such scanners are capable of scanning both prints and transparencies, up to the size of the input drum. Instead of using an array of CCDs that moves across the copy, the material to be scanned is placed on a clear acrylic drum that rotates underneath three photomultiplier tubes (PMTs). PMTs have a greater sensitivity range than CCDs and can detect a density range up to 3.8, which improves shadow definition. Resolutions of up to 5000 dpi support high enlargement percentages. RGB-to-CMYK conversion can be done by the host computer or by an optional circuit board containing a dedicated color computer.

High-end drum scanners are floor-model machines with large input drums, high-resolution PMT light detectors, and built-in color computers. High-end scanners can be programmed by a skilled operator for a multiplicity of settings that take printing conditions into consideration. These scanners have traditionally produced the highest quality work and offered the greatest productivity.

To simplify the operation of desktop drum, high-end drum, and professional-quality flatbed scanners, manufacturers have introduced software for automatic image processing. Such software analyzes the image and makes settings for the picture highlight, shadow, midtone, gray balance, and color correction. Using automated scanning software, it is possible to achieve better results with less training on scanner operation and color reproduction.

COPYDOT SCANNING AND DESCREENING

A common question from those considering computer-to-plate is what to do with film supplied by the customer. Certain plate systems can be exposed either in a platesetter or in a vacuum frame, enabling film to be incorporated into the layout. However, to real-

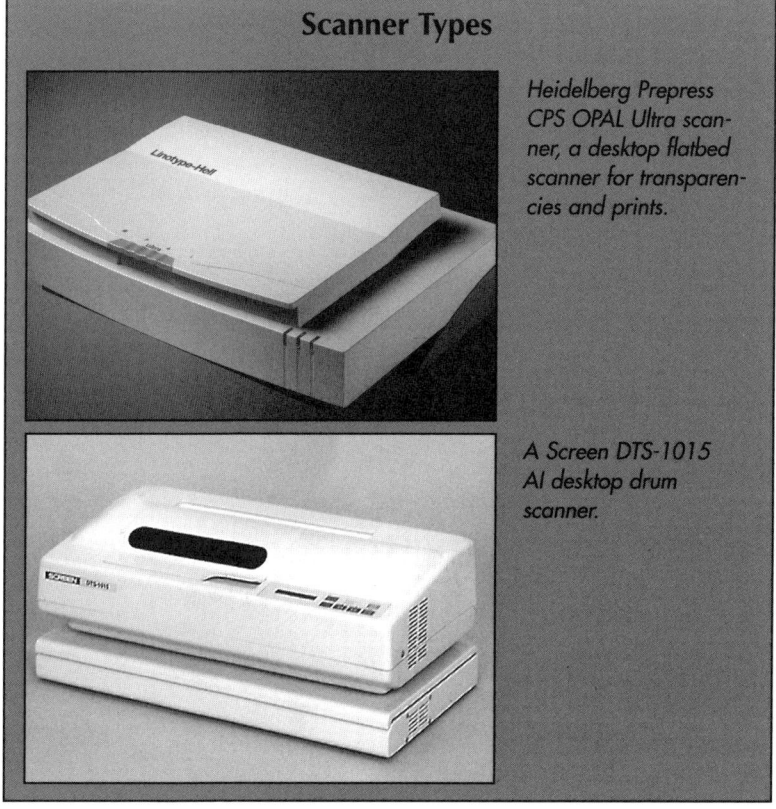

Scanner Types

Heidelberg Prepress CPS OPAL Ultra scanner, a desktop flatbed scanner for transparencies and prints.

A Screen DTS-1015 AI desktop drum scanner.

ize computer-to-plate's full potential for high quality, reduced cost, and faster turnaround, all work supplied should be in digital form. Two methods are used for converting black-and-white film to digital files. Copydot scanning refers to high-resolution scanning of black-and-white line work to create a high-resolution bitmapped image. Descreening is the process of scanning an existing halftone, whether on film or paper, be it one black-and-white halftone film or four color separations. A halftone, when rescanned, tends to develop moiré, an interference pattern created by the interaction of the two halftone patterns. To avoid moiré, descreening involves scanning the work slightly out of focus to blur the dot pattern. Descreening of halftones and color separations produces smaller files than copydot scanning.

SOFTWARE

One of the keys to desktop publishing was the development of page-layout software, computer programs for combining type and graphics. Today, the creation of pages involves the use of potentially many different software programs for creating pages, making line-art illustrations and diagrams, and scanning halftones and color separations—not to mention professional prepress activities such as imposition and trapping.

PAGE-LAYOUT PROGRAMS

Page layout refers to the creation of pages and the elements on them. Typically pages include typography in headlines and body type. They may also include borders, rules, and shaded or colored backgrounds.

A basic distinction between page-layout programs is batch versus interactive pagination. Batch mode is when the page-layout program assembles a complete document from start to finish by importing a word processing document. The program adds as many pages as necessary to contain the document, applying specified styles to the type. Interactive page layout refers to a designer manually creating each page and positioning the content on the page.

Page-layout software can also be object-oriented versus interactive. Object-oriented means that the user creates objects, such as text boxes and picture boxes, to hold the page elements like text and illustrations. Interactive means that these objects are placed freely on the page. Object-oriented programs make it easy to precisely control the position, size, and scaling of elements, whereas interactive programs are easier to use in batch-processing mode.

Current page-layout programs can import text from common word processing programs such as Microsoft Word, WordPerfect, and others, retaining the styles applied to text, headings, captions, and other elements. Page-layout programs import graphics conforming to encapsulated PostScript (EPS) and tagged image file format (TIFF) specifications.

Commonly the images imported into page layouts do not become part of the digital page-layout document. To help reduce the size of the page-layout file, they remain separate and are referred to as "linked graphics." The page layout program establishes a link to imported graphics and represents them with a low-resolution preview image on the screen. A common error in transmitting digital files to an output service is to omit linked graphics, resulting in the output of a low-resolution preview image in place of the high-resolution graphic file.

ILLUSTRATION SOFTWARE

Vector graphics. Illustration software refers mainly to programs used to create vector-graphic artwork, including diagrams and logos. Leading examples are Adobe Illustrator and Macromedia FreeHand. The advantages of vector graphics are scalability and small file size. Illustrations can be enlarged or reduced with no difference in image quality. Using equations to describe graphic elements results in small file sizes, as compared to comparable bitmapped images.

A potential disadvantage of vector graphic images is that each point and line in the image must be processed by the raster image processor (RIP) on output. Early-model RIPs sometimes lacked the processing power to handle the many lines and points of complex vector graphics, but as RIPs have become more powerful they have become better able to handle complex vector graphics.

Many vector-based drawing programs are able to import bitmapped images, including those in PICT, EPS, and TIFF formats. However, other than scaling, they are not able to perform image processing on bitmapped files.

Vector graphics are saved in native (i.e., the program's own) format or, for importation into page-layout software, in EPS format.

Bitmapped software. Bitmapped software is used primarily to make scans and do image editing, but it can also be used to create artwork. Examples include Adobe Photoshop, Fractal Painter, and proprietary scanning programs written for specific scanners. Bitmapped programs enable the user to "paint" a bitmapped graphic, using a variety of painter-like tool icons, including pencils, air brushes, and paint buckets. They also enable processing and retouching of scanned images, including changing the lightness, darkness, contrast, color balance, hue, and saturation of colors.

A bitmapped program can typically handle various bitmapped image modes, including line art, grayscale, RGB color, and CMYK color. Recent developments include the ability to handle device-independent CIE LAB color and Kodak's YCC Photo-CD format.

Bitmapped software can save files in native format or in TIFF, EPS, or PICT format. Compression may also be applied to bitmapped images, including JPEG (Joint Photographic Experts Group) compression to PICT and EPS images, and LZW (Lempel Ziv Welch) compression to TIFF images.

IMPOSITION AND TRAPPING PROGRAMS

Imposition—the positioning of pages on a press sheet so that, when folded, the pages will be in the correct sequence—has traditionally been visual and intuitive. But today there are a wide variety of imposition software programs that organize the required layout, remembering relevant information such as page position, numbering, measurements, margins and footers, and trim. These programs also make provisions for plate sizes, number of pages per plate, and print resizing for small-format proof output. Additionally, imposition programs allow users to create their own register marks, signatures, print and cutting commands in the correct size and location.

CTP does away with a number of traditional jobs which were used to compensate for the type of paper and inks used and the particular press characteristics that cause unprinted areas on the finished sheet. These adjustments will now come under the area of trapping, which is needed when misregister between the process color images creates unprinted areas in the finished print where colors should touch.

To compensate for this, either the inner image is enlarged or the outer image is reduced by a small amount. To do this electronically, the print process parameters have to be known and the corresponding settings have to be available on the computer screen for the operator to be able to make adjustments.

Single-page trapping is available with Adobe Photoshop and QuarkXPress. A number of add-on programs will do multipage trapping. Use the fastest computer available to run the trapping program. Be aware that the operator not only needs specific knowledge of the print parameters, but also a certain amount of patience even with the fastest processors.

Imposition and trapping are both discussed in more detail in a later chapter.

FILE PREPARATION AND PREFLIGHTING

FILE PREPARATION

Although PostScript is a common thread that runs through desktop publishing documents from scanning to output, the multiplicity of software programs, hardware platforms, and operators sometimes presents problems with consistency of file preparation.

In response to the growing use of desktop publishing as a means of document preparation, industry associations collaborated to write guidelines for file preparation. One such industry guideline is the Graphic Communication Association's (GCA) Electronic Mechanical Specification (EMS) published in 1991. Another specification was the Scitex Graphic Arts Users Association (SGAUA) Computer-Ready Electronic Files (CREF) guideline.

CREF represents the efforts of a number of printers, separators, and consultants to draft a set of guidelines for preparing desktop publishing files for successful output to film. These electronic mechanicals, artwork, and scanned imagery can be a cost-effective and efficient method of electronic prepress production—when produced correctly. They can also be a nightmare of overtime, excess charges, and missed press schedules when printers and separators are forced to troubleshoot files that have been built incorrectly. The goal of CREF is to provide suggestions to help minimize the chance of problems with files that one has created or is charged with outputting.

PREFLIGHTING

A term borrowed from the checklist procedures pilots use before taking off, preflighting is a way to make sure digital files will image properly. Computer-to-plate offers advantages of economy, turnaround, and quality compared to conventional production methods. When customers would hand their printers mechanical boards and photos, however, it was easy to tell whether the work was properly prepared and complete. With digital artwork, it is difficult to tell whether documents are properly prepared.

Preflighting is a way to discover problems before they tie up time, materials, and equipment. Preflighting is a process for analyzing a digital job for output readiness, regardless of the intended output device. It's a way to discover incomplete or missing digital files, missing fonts, improper or ignored trapping, inadequate bleeds, wrong page sizes, incorrect color breakdowns, extraneous elements, potential banding, jagged images, and other problems before a job is output. Font problems alone, considered the most troublesome aspect of proper output, justify preflighting. The preflighting process can involve the use of software or checklists or both.

A variety of programs are available to help service providers preflight files. Some programs reveal the most obvious errors by verifying fonts, graphics, colors, and page settings. Other programs verify that a file will RIP properly by RIPing to the screen or to a low-cost laser printer prior to RIPing on the platesetter or imagesetter.

FILE COMPRESSION

File compression reduces the size of files, which is important when transmitting files over phone lines or through networks. The two basic compression types are referred to as lossy, meaning that information is discarded but the files become smaller, and lossless, meaning that no information is lost but less compression occurs.

Among the two most common types of compression used in the graphic arts, the most popular is JPEG (Joint Photographic Experts Group). JPEG is a lossy compression commonly used on EPS- and PICT-type file formats. With lossy compression there is a direct relationship between the amount of compression, the amount of information discarded, and the reduction in file size. Different compression levels can be selected starting with a minimum of an 8:1 compression ratio. There are five JPEG compression options: high, medium-high, medium, medium-low, and low compression

JPEG-High yields high compression rates with noticeable loss in image quality while JPEG-Low compresses little but preserves image quality.

Lossless compression schemes do not suffer the same data loss that JPEG compression does. LZW/ZIP, CCITT Groups 3 & 4, and Run Length Encoded (RLE) are all lossless compressions, the most popular of which is LZW (named after the authors, Lempel, Ziv, and Welch). This type of compression is most popular with word processing text and can achieve 50% reduction in file size. It can also be applied to bitmapped images such as TIFF files but results in significantly less compression. Only LZW/ZIP can compress color, grayscale, and monochrome images. JPEG compression reduces network transmission time but, depending on the compression ratio, could result in lower quality. LZW compression doesn't jeopardize image quality but gives less compression and longer transmission times for operations with halftones and color separations.

Using data compression can significantly reduce idle waiting times and should be considered as a part of a company's overall system.

ACROBAT AND PDF FORMAT

Adobe Acrobat, currently in version 4.0, is a program developed for sharing documents across electronic networks. Using a simple program, Acrobat Reader, available on-line and free of charge, the end-user can open, read, and print out pages containing text, line art, and pictures. A companion program, Acrobat Distiller, is actually a software RIP that turns pages into Adobe's Portable Document Format (PDF), independent of the application, fonts, and platform on which they were created. Pages and the images they contain are compressed to accelerate electronic transmission. The PDF format has attracted attention from graphic arts users because of its platform independence, small file sizes, and hassle-free (i.e., pre-RIPed) output.

Document portability is our concern. Computer users have suffered from a lack of formatted text, loss of graphics, and lack of proper fonts needed to view and print documents. Documents have been somewhat portable through the use of ASCII and Rich Text Format (RTF) files, but content alone does not always convey the true message without formatting. Writing a file to PDF makes it "portable" across computer platforms. A PDF file is a 7-bit ASCII file, and uses only the printable subset of the ASCII set to describe documents—even those with images and special characters. Thus,

PDF files are portable even across diverse hardware and operating system environments.

CREATING A PDF FILE

The two methods for creating PDF are PDFWriter and Acrobat Distiller.

The PDFWriter, available on both Apple Macintosh computers and computers running the Microsoft Windows environment, acts as a printer driver. The PDFWriter shows up as a printer in the Macintosh Chooser window. The user needs to choose that "printer" to create a PDF file. The user then "prints" files to the PDFWriter and an electronic file is produced. This is similar to "print to disk."

For more complex documents that involve high-resolution images and detailed illustrations, the PDF file must be created differently because of limitations of PDFWriter. Acrobat Distiller was developed for this situation. Distiller produces PDF files from PostScript files that have been "printed to disk." The Distiller application accepts any PostScript file, whether created by a program or hand-coded.

NETWORKING AND DATA TRANSMISSION

The network is the electrical data connection between the various components. Both the type of connection and the physical layout of the network have to be taken into consideration. The topology will depend on spatial arrangements available and size. Networks tend to be star or ring-shaped arrangements, or a combination of the two. They can also be in a bus configuration, one computer linked to the next and on down the line. Network connections can be via simple telephone lines (which consist of two cables per line, referred to as twisted-pair cables), coaxial cables, or fiber-optic lines for high-volume demand work.

Networking is more than simply connecting computers together. Workstations are connected to each other, and to shared file servers and output devices. Computers can communicate with a RIP, or with a digital proofing device inhouse or across an ocean. Files can be sent to a laser printer on the desk next to you or to a digital printer for high-resolution final output. With today's increasingly digital workflow, networks are an integral part of every printer's setup.

As shorter and shorter deadlines become the expected norm in the printing industry, connectivity becomes even more important. Improved hardware, software, and telecommunications make data transfer faster and easier than it has been in the past.

Telecommunications also includes data transfer beyond a local area network. Transmission of digital files via high-speed phone lines complements computer-to-plate workflow because of its reduced turnaround time. Advantages of digital transmission are that it's faster than shipping disks by courier; it costs less to deliver the files, especially considering the savings in copying, packing, and shipping disks; and, files can be sent any time of the day, without concern over pickup schedules. Disadvantages include the inability to accompany digital files with physical materials, including proofs, films, ads, or artwork. Also, the transmission process ties up two computers: one at the sending site and one at the receiving site.

Telecommunications and online services make it possible to offer customers many options, including delivery of digital files, access to files stored on the print shop's server, the ability to print directly from a customer's workstation to an output device at the printer's, searchable databases such as job jacket information from previous jobs or archived images, and scheduling information on job progress.

3 Raster Image Processing

At the heart of any digital workflow are the raster image processor (RIP), which does most of the work in preparing files for actual output, and the server, which acts as data warehouse and traffic cop for the system. Every major supplier of imagesetters has introduced higher-performance RIPs, as well as an architecture for data control and flow from workstations and input devices to a plethora of output devices. Almost all RIP/servers support OPI or other automatic picture replacement approaches, where high-resolution images are maintained at the server while low-resolution images are used for page assembly. The low-res files are then replaced by the high-res files when the job is sent to the RIP.

With the advent of computer-to-plate and computer-to-digital press, the RIP/server becomes even more important as users implement digital workflow. RIPs are evolving into RIP management systems. A major goal is to RIP once and then output to multiple digital devices. This allows the same RIPed file to drive both a digital color proofer and a CTP system, for instance.

HARLEQUIN SCRIPTWORKS

Since a majority of CTP systems utilize Harlequin's ScriptWorks RIP management system, we thought it appropriate to include a description of it. It competes with Agfa's Apogee and Heidelberg's Delta workflows.

ScriptWorks 5.0, sold exclusively to OEM partners, can process files produced by applications compliant with the PostScript 3 specification, and it supports the full range of new PostScript 3 operators as well as earlier versions of the language.

More than a PostScript language interpreter and rasterizer, ScriptWorks can process a wide variety of file formats, from PostScript, PDF, and EPS to TIFF 6 and TIFF/IT-P1. It lets you choose the tools and workflows you want to incorporate in products to meet your customers' needs.

ScriptWorks outputs 4,096 levels of gray in gradient fills using Harlequin Precision Screening (HPS). "Extra grays" can make output from even low-resolution devices smoother and more sophisticated.

With Harlequin Color Production Solutions (HCPS), ScriptWorks delivers color-matching capability with optimal efficiency. HCPS is a suite of color-processing options for ScriptWorks. The HCPS products use an in-RIP color engine and provide ICC "device-link" color support to conform to the latest industry standards. Built-in color management ensures that each color is not only rendered accurately, but also consistently—whether within a single job or across multiple printings.

Users can process multiple jobs simultaneously with pipeline processing. As one file is input, another is interpreted and a third is output. The output device may run at full engine speed, without stopping between pages or jobs.

Symmetrical multiprocessing (SMP) support lets you achieve tremendous speed and increase throughput by processing multiple parts of a job simultaneously on a multiprocessor server.

SCRIPTWORKS FEATURES

Full platform compatibility. ScriptWorks runs on industry standard hardware platforms and operating systems. Its feature set, source code, and user interface are consistent, no matter which platform you use.

Support for graphics formats. ScriptWorks can produce halftone output, 8-bit grayscale output, 8- and 10-bit run-length encoded

(RLE) output, and color contone (continuous-tone) output in CMYK and RGB formats. It supports all-raster workflows (to drive raster output devices such as proof printers) and drives contone color printers as well as imagesetters, platesetters, and direct imaging presses. In addition to printing output conventionally, ScriptWorks can also print raster files to disk. This capability enables users to produce documents in formats such as TIFF.

Unlimited file formats. Users can process virtually any input file format, including PostScript, JPEG, DCS 2, EPS, TIFF 6, and TIFF/IT-P1.

Input plug-ins control and define input in PostScript language, PDF, and a variety of raster formats from virtually any external source using ScriptWorks' input plug-in technology. ScriptWorks ships with a series of standard input plug-ins.

CIP3 support. Harlequin now offers a CIP3 plug-in for ScriptWorks that is the first step toward software-based links between prepress, press, and postpress operations in a printing workflow. Harlequin's CIP3 plug-in enables end users to automatically include press-specific ink key setting data in a RIPed file. This data is then provided to the press operator as a PPF version 2 file (low-resolution preview file). When the PPF file is read by a CIP3 reader (as provided with press control systems) it will provide instructions for automatically setting ink fountains on press, thereby saving the press operator time, minimizing errors, and reducing waste.

Extensive font support. ScriptWorks supports all PostScript font types, including Types 0, 1, 3, 4, and 42 formats. ScriptWorks comes loaded with 35 standard fonts, plus several extra system fonts. You can choose to extend the supplied font set for your customers and easily load additional fonts into the RIP.

Media management. ScriptWorks allows the user to keep track of available media on up to 16 input cassettes and receive a warning when media runs low. ScriptWorks can automatically choose the most media-efficient orientation for each job or it can let the user dictate page position.

Last-minute checks and balances. ScriptWorks includes a "late-binding" approach to workflow management. With late-binding technology, device-dependent decisions—about trapping, color management and so on—are postponed until the output device has been designated. You have the flexibility to make these irrevocable or "binding" decisions at the last possible moment.

Job preview. Remakes can be reduced by quickly RIPing a job and checking for errors on screen before final processing.

Automatic recovery. ScriptWorks' Throughput Controller allows the user to compress and store rasterized jobs to disk before directing them to the output device. Then additional copies or a new separation film can be output without interpreting the page again.

Output control. The output control in ScriptWorks allows the user to reorder pages, abort printing of selected pages midstream, and reprint pages without reinterpreting the original page.

Harlequin Color Production Solutions. Harlequin Color Production Solutions (HCPS) is a suite of options for handling color process control. They work with industry standard ICC 3 profiles and have full "device-link" capability.

Harlequin screening library. Allows the user to achieve unprecedented precision and clarity with high- and low-resolution applications. This collection of advanced screening techniques includes a wide range of screen rulings, special angles, and dot shapes, including Harlequin Dispersed Screening (HDS), a patented "FM" (stochastic) screening option.

POSTSCRIPT

PostScript is a page-description language developed and licensed by Adobe Systems, Inc. for describing elements to be output on digital printers. PostScript is a device-independent page description language; it can be used to describe output on any printer, regardless of its resolution. The device independence of PostScript has enabled computer platforms, software, and output devices from many different manufacturers to work together in creating digital pages. Adobe licenses PostScript to RIP and printer manufacturers; it does not need to be purchased by the user.

When sending out PostScript files, make sure (where at all possible) that the whole file is supplied with the program it was created in, e.g., PageMaker, rather than in pure PostScript files, which need to be processed before they can be displayed on the screen. PostScript is just a long list of instructions that the connected RIP recognizes and converts into pixel patterns that can be viewed by the human eye.

A key feature of PostScript is its ability to handle both vector and bitmapped images. A vector image, as might be created in Adobe Illustrator or Macromedia FreeHand, is described by mathematical equations that determine the shape of lines. Vector graphic images are device-independent and scalable. Bitmapped graphics, on the other hand, have a specified resolution based on picture elements, or pixels, of specified bit depth (the "bit" in bitmapped), arranged in an x-y coordinate system (the "map" in bitmapped).

POSTSCRIPT INTERPRETERS AND RIPS

When the RIP receives the PostScript file for processing, it needs to convert that file to bitmap data. PostScript printers, whether 300-dpi laser printers or 3000+ dpi platesetters, need a PostScript interpreter to translate the PostScript code into the bilevel bitmap data needed to image the page. Raster data prints a page as a pattern of tiny printer dots or spots. To place these dots, the RIP maps out the page as a grid of spot locations—called a bitmap.

Bitmap data is what the output engine or recorder needs. But PostScript really describes pages not as a table of spots, but as a series of mathematically described shapes or objects. It takes a lot less data to describe a page by its shape, size, and location than by listing the state (on or off) of each individual spot, dot, or pixel in the image. The PostScript interpreter converts the PostScript code to a list of objects. Then it rasterizes the objects to create the bitmap for actual outputting. The resolution of the output device determines how many spots are needed to image a page.

The RIP, or raster image processor, is really the PostScript programming language compiler. It interprets the file and "executes" its commands, which are to draw objects on a page. A RIP is the essential element in any form of raster-based imaging. The end result of RIPing is a rasterized bitmap image that tells the output engine where to place dots. The RIP performs five functions:

1. Interpretation of the page description language code from the application program
2. Display list generation
3. Rasterizing (making the bitmap)
4. Trapping
5. Screening

Almost every imaging device available today is a raster imager—using spots to build text, lines, photos, etc. Thus, every imager must, out of necessity, have a RIP, whether it is a lowly desktop printer or a giant computer-to-plate system.

PDF-BASED PRODUCTION SYSTEMS

The high-speed data requirements of digital presses, large-format film imposetters, and computer-to-plate systems demand radical changes in RIP and workflow architectures. Developers are also trying to eliminate PostScript processing bottlenecks and accelerate deadline production times. Demands for last-minute changes in pages foster a concept known as "late binding." RIP developers are working toward a format that allows data to be changed after it has been interpreted by the RIP. These changes take account of different printing requirements, proofing requirements, or nonprint delivery. RIP suppliers have been converting PostScript into contone (CT) and linework (LW) files via proprietary methods or converting

PostScript into some editable internal format in an attempt to make the RIPing process more efficient.

In contrast with the bitmap or vector formats, the object-based PDF is slim and smart. Slim because, unlike the complex, continuous data stream in a PostScript file, it consists of a compact—or distilled—object-oriented database of imaging operations that can immediately represent the document on a page-by-page level. Job Ticket information, part of the PDF file, lets you store and manage device-dependent information, independent from job content.

Adobe's Extreme RIP architecture is built around Adobe's Portable Document Format. PostScript is an interpretive programming language; PDF is a compact, noninterpretive format designed for fast imaging to a screen. PDF has lacked the ability to handle high-resolution images easily and to handle screening for print—both of these are included within Extreme. Multipage jobs can be processed by several RIPs simultaneously. Extreme is aimed primarily at high-volume applications.

SCREENING

The process in which a continuous-tone image is converted into a halftone is called screening. The conversion from photographic image to a matrix of dots allows for the outputting of halftones along with type and color separations.

RATIONAL TANGENT (RT) SCREENING®

The first type of PostScript screening, RT screening, was introduced by Linotype-Hell with the RIP 1 and was licensed to other RIP manufacturers. The RT screening process angled the screens by defining the angle of rotation in terms of discrete (rational) numbers on a reference grid of horizontal and vertical image spots.

When making color separations, screen angles must be rotated 30° between colors to avoid screen moiré patterns. Moiré is an unintended and unwanted optical effect that results from an out-of-register overlap of patterns. Screen angles of 1°, 15°, 45°, and 75° are commonly used for four-color separations. RT screening can define angles of 0° and 45° precisely. However, RT screening cannot precisely define angles of 15° and 75° because the tangents of 15° and 75° are not whole numbers.

SUPERCELL SCREENING

To more accurately define screen angles, several RIP manufacturers developed screening algorithms that define the screen angle using a larger-scale reference grid of image pixels. This larger reference grid, called a "supercell," actually extends outside of the boundaries of individual halftone dot cells.

Supercell screening reduces the tendency for screen moiré in four-color separations by more precisely defining the 15° and 75° angles. One disadvantage of supercell screening is that it requires more computational power than RT screening due to the larger size of the reference grid, but with the high processing speeds of today's RIPs, this is not a significant problem.

FM OR STOCHASTIC SCREENING

Stochastic or frequency-modulated (FM) screening, on the other hand, creates the illusion of tones with variably spaced dots. First-order stochastic screens vary only the spacing of uniformly sized dots.

Printers are still debating its pros and cons. FM advocates point to the absence of subject moiré (interference patterns created by imposing a conventional screening pattern on an existing subject pattern, such as woven fabric), better rendition of detail and tone, and greater tolerance of misregistration. Detractors of FM screening point to the steep learning curve involved in dealing with higher dot gain on press and the precise exposure control needed for proofing and platemaking.

Although studies are either rare or not well publicized, computer-to-plate should offer a solution to some of stochastic screening's drawbacks. With negative-working plates and 150-lpi screen ruling, the extra imaging step of exposing film to plate results in an additional 3—12% dot gain. Platesetters, of course,

> **Screening Rules to Avoid Moiré**
>
> - Try to separate each color from the next by 30°.
> - Where this is not possible, separate them by at least 15°.
> - Make all halftones the same screen ruling.
> - Set cyan to 15°, black to 45°, magenta to 75°, and yellow to 0°.
> - Move black to 75° and magenta to 45° if the image contains important flesh tones. (This avoids a conflict between magenta and yellow.)
> - Move black to 15° and cyan to 45° if the image is predominantly light green. (This avoids a cyan and yellow conflict.)
> - In three-color (CMY) work, or in cases where black does not play a dominant role, consider shifting yellow to 45°.
>
> * Jim Hamilton, *Moiré*, Technical Information, Linotype-Hell Company. Part No. 3063, 1991.

eliminate the film step and its extra generation of dot gain, and they can be calibrated for accurate screen reproduction.

The choice of plates will likely impact the success of stochastic screening in a computer-to-plate environment. Plates that have the highest resolutions and best image stability would most likely give the best results with FM screening.

ELECTRONIC TRAPPING

Trap, a slight overlap of adjacent colors, is necessary to compensate for possible press misregister, and to avoid unwanted lines between colors. In conventional stripping, trapping is done by contacting or duplicating films using overexposure, clear spacer sheets, and other techniques to enlarge ("spread") or reduce ("choke") images and create necessary overlaps.

Electronic trapping methods are an important consideration in a multicolor computer-to-plate workflow. Electronic trapping can be divided into four categories, based on where the trapping occurs.

Manual illustration trapping. Designers can create traps in illustration software, such as Adobe Illustrator or Macromedia FreeHand, by specifying object fills and overprinting strokes. Although easier than conventional trapping, manual illustration trapping has the following drawbacks:
- Manual trapping is time-consuming.
- To trap manually, an artist must know the graphic's reproduction percentage.
- A designer should create traps based on the screen ruling, printing methods, and press that will be used for the job.

Application trapping. This method refers to the automatic trapping features of QuarkXPress and Adobe PageMaker software, in which page-layout objects are trapped. Application trapping can be easier than manual illustration trapping. Drawbacks are:
- Application trapping requires learning additional software features.
- Application trapping features trapping for page-layout objects only, not imported graphics.

Dedicated trapping programs. Software like Imation TrapWise, DK&A Trapper, and Ultimate TrapEze operate on EPS files after they are created by an application and before they are RIPed. These programs can overcome the limitations of application trapping and make it possible to trap complex objects that would be impossible to trap conventionally or manually. However, using a dedicated trapping program requires a separate production step and perhaps an additional workstation.

RIP-based software. Software like Scitex Full Auto-Frames and RAMPAGE operates at the RIP level to trap files. RIP-based trapping programs are the most powerful and most expensive electronic trapping solutions, but they may be worthwhile for high-volume production like that associated with computer-to-plate production.

IMPOSITION

Imposition, also sometimes referred to as stripping or image assembly, is the process of laying out the various components of a page before printing and arranging them so that they will fold correctly. Imposition might be described as the brain teaser of print production. You must not only consider product size with paper stock, paper thickness, press sheet size, signature size, equipment capacities, and image registration, but you must also position and orient the pages to read right-side up and in the correct sequence after the book is finished.

Imposition is an important part of planning any book, booklet, magazine, manual, catalog, etc. How you design and produce a book will depend upon the choice of imposition—a choice that, in turn, will be limited by the capabilities of printing and bindery equipment. Some of the production variables that influence the choice of imposition for books of four or more pages include product size, page count, and paper size.

To print a book of a given size and page count requires a certain number of signatures of a specified paper size. Other production variables include the size capacity of the printing presses, folders, and binding machines to be used.

Printing presses are commonly described by their width and cylinder circumference (repeat length). Duplicators usually run paper lengthwise, and presses run paper widthwise. Larger presses cost more to operate than smaller presses, but they can print more pages faster.

After printing, large, multiple-page press sheets are commonly folded one, two, or more times by folding machines. The folds can be perpendicular to each other (right-angle folds) or in the same direction (parallel folds). Folding machines, like presses, come in different sizes, and are usually matched to accommodate the largest printable sheet size.

IMAGE REGISTER AND ALIGNMENT

An imposition plan should consider the mechanism of sheet travel through the press. Lithographic presses, which are more precise than offset duplicators, align sheets against the leading edge and one side. This alignment can be critical to image registration and alignment, particularly if the paper is not precisely square.

Gripper edge. Before each sheet passes between the press cylinders, it is stopped momentarily and its leading edge is aligned with the press grippers, which pull the sheet into the press. The leading edge of the sheet is therefore called the gripper edge and is the most precise line of head-to-tail alignment. Due to its importance to registration and alignment, printers commonly mark the gripper edge on imposition diagrams with an "x."

Side guide. As the sheet passes from the infeed toward the gripper edge, it is jogged toward one side of the press against a side guide, the most precise edge of side-to-side alignment on the sheet. Printers commonly mark the side guide edge with a short straight line.

IMPOSITION PLANS

In production planning, consideration must be given to a number of possible scenarios, starting at the press, which will affect both post- and prepress planning:
- Is the sheet flipped side-to-side or top-to-bottom when it is backed up?
- How many plates, or forms, will be required to print each press sheet on the front and back?
- How many copies are printed at one time on each press sheet, whether two at a time (two-up), four at a time (four-up), and so on?
- How many passes through the press (impressions) are required to print the job?

Sheetwise

With a sheetwise imposition, the press operator has a separate set of plates for the front and back of each press sheet; hence, two plates are required for each printing unit. After printing the first side, side "A," the operator must back up the sheets, turning them upside down by flipping them from side to side. Then side "B" is printed with the separate set of plates. The gripper edge remains the same when the sheets are backed up. With single side-guide presses, however, the side guide ends up on the opposite side of the sheet.

A press sheet can be imposed sheetwise, one-up or more. With a two-up imposition, the press sheets would need to be cut in half after the pressrun, but only half the press sheets and printing impressions would be required, which would save press time. This imposition is generally used if the front and back of a piece are dissimilar, as with a four-color front and a one-color back, or if any special treatments, such as varnishing or coating, will be done to one side only.

Work-and-Turn

Work-and-turn is a clever, if puzzling, imposition allowing the printer to print the front and back and get two-up signatures all from one set of plates: side "A" on the right, side "B" on the left. When the sheets are flipped side to side and backed up, front side "A" gets backed up with side "B"; front side "B" gets backed up with side "A." The press operator winds up with two identical, backed-up images. As with sheetwise imposition, the gripper edge remains the same, but the side guide moves to the other side.

This imposition generally saves time and materials, since separate plates for front and back are not needed. Generally, this imposition is also the fastest in the pressroom, since adjustments to the press after the first pass are minimal. One of the drawbacks to this imposition is that the ink must be dry enough before the sheets can be run through the press again.

Basic Sheetfed Impositions

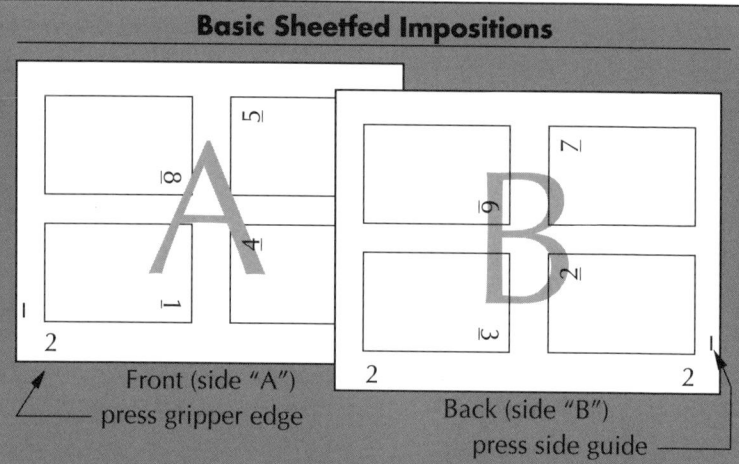

Front (side "A")
press gripper edge

Back (side "B")
press side guide

SHEETWISE
(Also called work-and-back, front-and-back, print-and-back)
- *2 plates: one front ("A"), one back ("B")*
- *Gripper edge remains the same*
- *Side guide moved to other side*

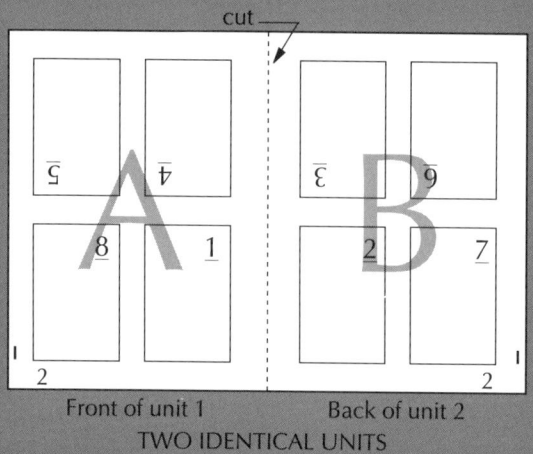

Front of unit 1   Back of unit 2
TWO IDENTICAL UNITS

WORK-AND-TURN
(Also called print-and-turn)
- *Print both sides with one plate; sheet will have 2 units, each one-half sheet; cut apart after printing*
- *Gripper edge remains the same*
- *Side guide moved to other side*

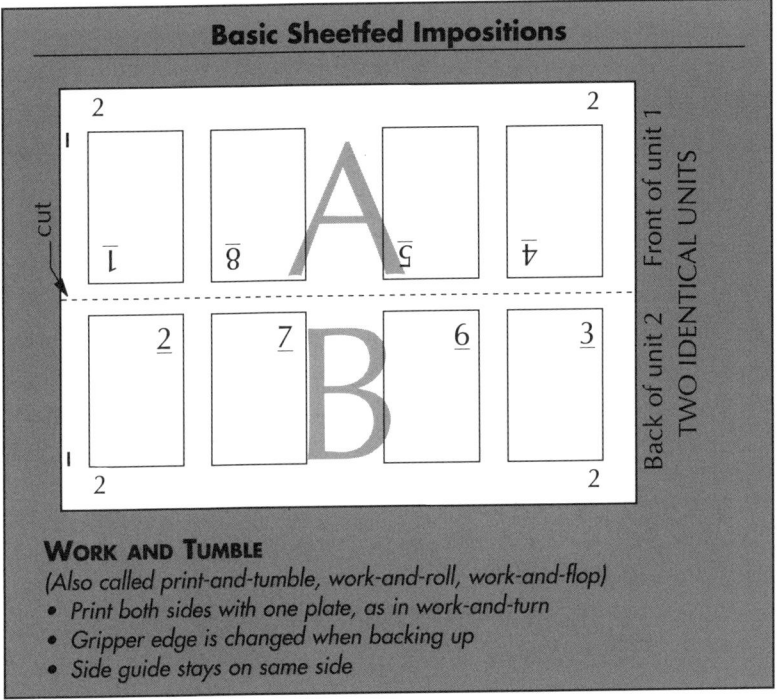

WORK-AND-TUMBLE

A variant of work-and-turn, the work-and-tumble imposition involves flipping the press sheets from head to tail before backing them up. This allows the side guide to remain the same but switches the gripper edges.

For this imposition, an extra allowance of paper must be factored in since the gripper edge changes head-to-tail. This is the imposition usually required for perfecting presses that can print both sides of the sheet with one pass through the press.

ALLOWANCES AND MARGINS

While planning an imposition, you need to allow extra paper for the printing press and binding machines, including press gripper margins, signature creep, binding machine lips, and trim allowances.

Gripper margin. Allowance must also be made for the area where the press gripper mechanism holds the sheet. This gripper margin varies from press to press, but is commonly ¼–½ in.

Creep. In thick books stapled through the spine (saddle stitched), the paper thickness tends to push the inner signatures away from the spine, which can result in diminishing outer margins toward the center of the book. Production planners leave allowances for such creep, depending upon the page count and paper thickness. This allowance is determined by the number of signatures, the number of folds per signature, and the caliper of the paper.

Trim allowances. After a press sheet is folded into a signature, one or more edges (in addition to the bind fold) will likely be closed, making the pages unopenable. After binding, the books are trimmed on three sides, making the edges uniform and resulting in the book's final size. Allowances for such trim margins must be included in the imposition. Generally, ⅛-in. trim allowances are sufficient.

Lips. If a book is to be bound on an automatic saddle-stitching machine, which opens the book and "staples" (stitches) it through the spine, an extension or lip is usually required to enable the binding machine to open the folded signature prior to stitching. Generally, a ¼-in. lip must be included in the imposition. Depending upon the saddle-stitching machine, the lip must be on the high- or low-folio side of each signature.

IMPOSITION SOFTWARE

As the printing industry tries to move toward an all-digital workflow, the art of stripping is being replaced by digital imposition. Digital imposition is typically divided into two categories: PostScript imposition software and RIP-based imposition solutions.

PostScript imposition. PostScript imposition software can operate within page-layout software (i.e., DK&A INposition functions as a

Quark XTension), creating paginated PostScript. Other programs are stand-alone software that work with previously created, unpaginated PostScript and EPS files to create a single, paginated PostScript document.

RIP-based imposition. In a typical PostScript workflow, PostScript data going to the RIP would contain data for multiple pages, with comments attached to position pages as needed. RIP-based imposition, though, works with the basic PostScript—without pagination information—to impose single pages after processing.

There are three basic types of RIP-based imposition:

1. Incoming PostScript, EPS, TIFF, or PDF files are processed into some unrasterized intermediate format, which is then imposed into a single document. That document is then rasterized, screened, and output.
2. PostScript, EPS, TIFF, PDF, and CEPS documents can be processed by the RIP into a series of independent raster files. Those files are then gathered, imposed, and screened during the output process.
3. PostScript, EPS, TIFF, PDF, or other document files can be processed at the RIP into independent, screened single pages. Those pages can then be combined and positioned for imposed output.

Whichever system you use, in- and post-RIP imposition offer certain benefits to an all-digital workflow. Page content can be changed easily, and only that page would have to be reRIPed (compared to reRIPing, say, a 400-page book because the image on page 173 was out of line). Aside from the benefit of allowing last-minute single-page changes, this also reduces the possibility that previously accepted pages might process incorrectly the second time.

4 PROOFING

One of the key questions in CTP production is how to proof the color separations and page layouts before making plates. Thus, digital proofing is an important enabling technology for CTP workflow. While many publishers rely on film-based, or laminated, proofs such as Imation Matchprint, DuPont Waterproof, Fuji Color-Art, or Enco Pressmatch, these methods cannot be used without film. Fortunately, digital proofing systems have been gaining in popularity, due to better color accuracy, faster turnaround, and greater acceptance by customers.

It can be argued that with a full CTP system in place, whatever is put into the system in digital form at the front end will emerge at the other end in the exact plate equivalent. As long as the customer's input is correct, that is what should happen. Unfortunately, this is not always the case. The solution, seen from the manufacturers' point of view, is to satisfy the proofing requirement of both printer and customer by using existing economical output devices in two operations.

- To provide a black-and-white "blueline" proof for positioning, etc., just prior to platemaking
- For commercial printing, a color proof which will provide a color check

Both these proofs should ideally be produced from the same RIP that will be used to produce the plates, thereby ensuring total accuracy, but this is going to take up precious recorder time while the proofs are being produced. It will be a matter of personal assessment, according to your business, whether you go this route or invest in separate recorder/proofer. A number of U.S. printers are already gaining acceptance from their customers for continuous-tone (contone or CT) proofs by offering faster turnaround. The areas to be addressed when considering CTP proofing will include:

1. Do you need a separate RIP for proofing or can you use the same RIP? If you use the same RIP as for your total system, will it mean that you will take time out of plate production while it is being used for proofing? If you use a separate RIP, there is additional expenditure as well as the potential for bothersome error when dealing with specially created fonts.
2. What is the customer requirement for black-and-white proofer positioning and layout? The larger the recorder, the more expensive it will be, and if you can get your customers to accept scaled-down black-and-white proofs, it will be quicker and cheaper for both of you.
3. What will the customer accept for color proofing, in terms of quality and size? You will probably have to undertake a certain amount of customer education when approaching this question, possibly even with your customer's customer (an ad agency or publisher, for example).

As more of what has been thought of as traditional prepress functions (page layout, scanning, and image manipulation) has become distributed to content providers, the need for accurate color communication between content and service provider has become more critical. All of the potential savings in time and material as well as the advantage of creative control are realized only if both the content and service providers have a reliable, accurate method to verify that their digital information will be output to film, plate, and press in the manner they expect. The digital proof becomes the critical communication tool between these two parties. The successful use of a digital proofing system to meet this need demands that two major criteria are met. First, the system must be able to produce color results that are accurate enough to ensure proper completion of the job. Second, the system must not be so expensive, complicated, or maintenance-intensive that it becomes unusable by the content provider.

BLACK-AND-WHITE PROOFING

Since, with CTP, films are not imaged and imposition is not done manually, a layout proof will be needed prior to imaging the plate. According to existing users in the market, this should be proof/plate size, driven by the same RIP that drives the platesetter to ensure optimum predictability, and can probably utilize a thermal, laser, or inkjet printer outputting at 400 dpi. There are a number of PostScript recorders available in the market ranging from A4 (8.27×11.69 in.) up to A1 (23.39×33.11 in.) and really, the decision is dictated by what your customer will accept.

COLOR DIGITAL PROOFING

"True" digital color proofing systems, i.e., those producing a conventional halftone dot from digital input, tend to be expensive—$150,000 to $300,000—and relatively slow.

There is debate about the need for "true" digital proofs. Prior to DuPont Cromalin, wet-press proofs could be obtained at considerable cost. When Cromalin came to the market, it was said that it would never be accepted because it didn't have the same quality as wet-press proofs. Then the market found out the savings that could be made using Cromalin proofs. Today's CTP user faces a very similar situation. Contone is making rapid strides in all areas of proofing and, with some customer education, inkjet, dye sublimation, and even electronic printing may overcome the initial negative reaction to accepting something other than halftone proofs. The following are some typical color systems available for digital proofing.

Photographic proofing. Using conventional photographic paper, a tricolor exposure device, and liquid developer, the traditional range of high-capital-cost, low-copy-cost machines include products from Dainippon Screen, Linotype-Hell, and Kodak.

Thermal transfer. These have traditionally been low-resolution systems employing dithered halftones to average out the image, but offer good line and text resolution at affordable cost. Normally used for concept or pre-proofing, the systems are cheap with low-cost proof copies.

Dye diffusion. This produces a contone output that provides a potential excellent press match and is proving to be the fastest growing product sector in digital proofing.

Inkjet. Systems using randomized dot to achieve a halftone effect are typically in the hands of Iris Graphics, owned by Scitex, and DuPont. These are the top-of-the-range systems.

Laser dye diffusion. The Kodak Approval system, outputting at 1800 dpi, laminates halftone dot proofs to actual paper stock to be used, employing a thermal laser dye transfer system. The Japanese market requirement for multiple contract proofs gives rise to a unique demand for large-format, high-quality output. The new digital color proofer from Screen outputs a 26×31-in. (660×787-mm) proof at either 2000 or 4000 dpi.

Pictrography. Fuji's FirstLook uses a silver halide donor material and a receiver material. The donor material is exposed simultaneously with three laser diodes. The exposed material is passed over distilled water that acts as a developing agent to activate the exposed dyes. Once activated the dyes are thermally transferred to one of three receivers, a matte, a gloss, and/or a transparency material, creating a photographic type print using only distilled water. The Pictrography system uses a silver halide-based semidry system to produce photo-quality contone proofs for the lower volume end of the market.

Thin-layer thermal transfer. Fuji's FirstProof uses a pre-coated CMYK color ribbon along with a receiver/transfer material that allows the proof to be laminated to actual printing paper. The technology uses the same CMYK pigments as Fuji's Color-Art analog proofing system to create the CMYK colors. Using pigments, not dyes, to create the CMYK colors gives the final output proof the same metameric characteristics as an analog proof or a press sheet.

Electrostatic. There is a growing potential for using xerographic color copiers as proofers. Color copiers with RIPs like the Xerox Majestik and the Canon CLC500 series output PostScript files as a proofer. Like the Canon system, the Majestik distinguishes between images and characters while scanning.

DOTS VERSUS NO DOTS

The ideal digital proof would be one that showed a dot pattern identical to the one that is imaged on the plate, and that could be closely calibrated to simulate the ink and paper conditions, including settings for density, tone reproduction, and gray balance. Digital proofers that show dots include the Kodak Approval, Polaroid PolaProof, and Screen TrueRite.

Many users express concern over seeing dots in proofs because they want to be assured that moiré patterns will not occur in printed subjects. Two types of moiré are subject moiré and screen moiré. Subject moiré, which arises from interaction between the halftone-dot screen pattern and patterns in subjects such as tweed fabrics, is a valid reason for wanting to see a proof with dots. Screen moiré, which occurs due to the inability of early PostScript RIPs to precisely angle screens 30° apart, has been mostly eliminated with today's "supercell" screening technology that enables RIPs to precisely set screen angles and hence avoid screen moiré.

Thanks to color calibration and color management software, most digital proofers now can be adjusted to simulate different printing conditions.

Whatever technology you choose, the crucial step is to build customer confidence in the new technology by showing consistent, high-quality digital proofs. In many cases, the best approach is to make both digital and photomechanical proofs during the transition period. This provides internal verification that the digital

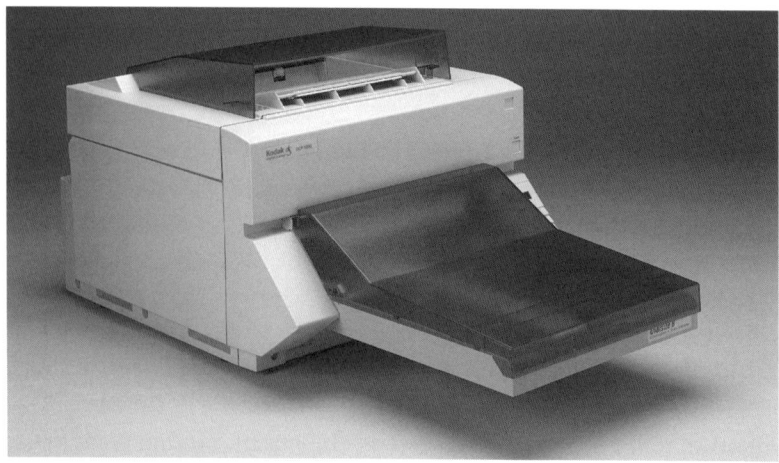

Kodak Polychrome Graphics DCP 9300 thermal dye diffusion proofer

proofs are consistent and high-quality, while allaying customer concerns that digital proofs are inherently inferior.

IMAGING TECHNOLOGIES

Thermal transfer. In thermal transfer, wax containing colored pigments is melted and sprayed in varying-size droplets onto wax-receptive paper. The wax colorants and paper are low in cost, resulting in a low cost for thermal transfer proofs. However, the wax pigments often have color gamuts different from those of typical offset printing, so color matching may not be good. Also, the proofs have a grainy appearance due to the individual colorant droplets, but the grain pattern does not correspond to halftone dots on the printed sheet.

Dye sublimation. Dye sublimation proofers use a thermal head with thousands of heating elements and a roll or ribbon containing CMYK colorants in a repeating pattern. In response to varying (up to 256) heat levels from the print head, colorant material sublimates (vaporizes from a solid state) from the ribbon and condenses onto a special paper or transparency receiver stock. Instead of a solid dot, dye sublimation printers produce bursts of color that are denser in the center and feathered toward the edges. When all four process colors are applied, each color blends into the next, producing a continuous-tone or photographic appearance.

Inkjet. Inkjet proofers spray dots of liquid ink onto the page. Although paper costs are lower than with dye sublimation proofers, inkjet technology is more expensive and requires more maintenance.

Laser, thermal/photographic. High-resolution, halftone-dot laser proofers including the Kodak Approval, Optronics IntelliProof, and Screen TrueRite use lasers to create halftone dots on dye-containing donor material or photographic emulsion by various proprietary methods.

ASSESSING PRINT CHARACTERISTICS OF DIGITAL PROOFERS

The decision whether a digital proof will serve as a satisfactory predictor of color appearance on press involves many characteristics that can be evaluated both visually and quantitatively. One of the best ways to assess the color reproduction characteristics of a particular digital proofer is to ask for a sample page to be imaged that contains test images as well as photographs, such as the GATF Digital Test Form.

Tone reproduction. To visually assess tone reproduction characteristics, which affect lightness, darkness, and contrast, examine highlight and shadow dots (assuming the proofer produces dots) with a magnifier or loupe. Notice the minimum and maximum printing dots, and determine whether these correspond to those of the press sheet.

Dot gain is best evaluated densitometrically, but dot gain can be visually evaluated by noting the relative lightness/darkness of tone scales and the balance of contrast between highlights and shadows on tone scales or in images. Ideally, a proofer should be able to distinguish between the 10% steps of a 0–100% tone scale.

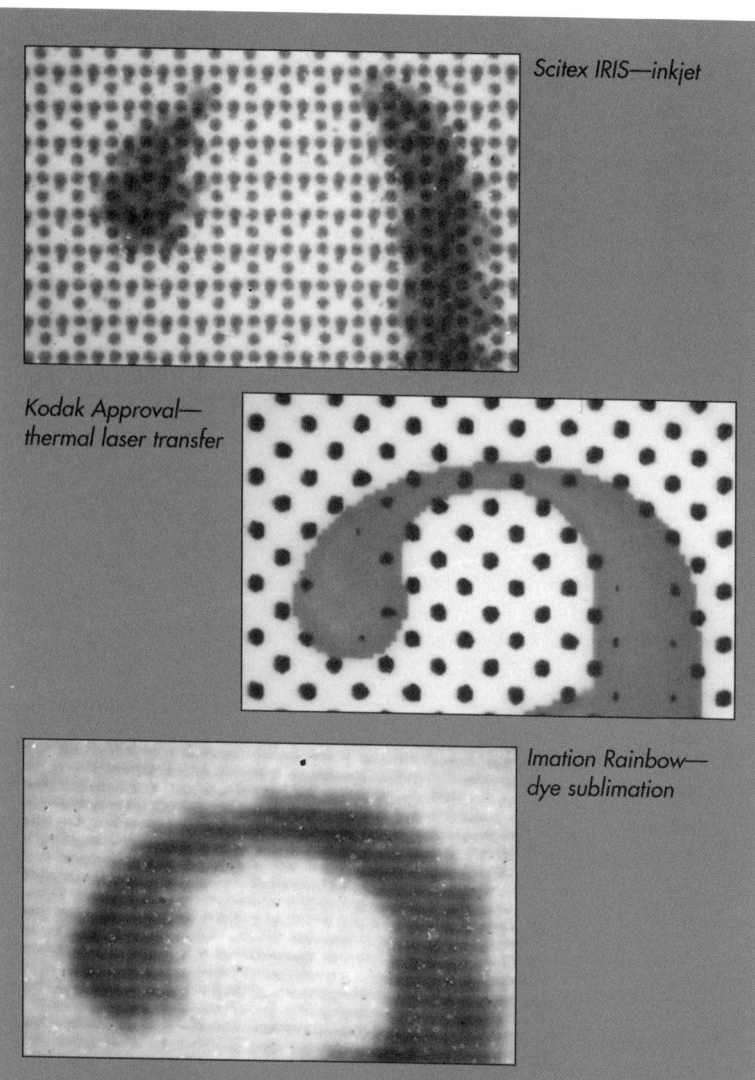

Scitex IRIS—inkjet

Kodak Approval—thermal laser transfer

Imation Rainbow—dye sublimation

50× photomicrographs of a 15% gray background (dots) trapped to a 9-pt. cyan letter "a" show the differences between laser thermal transfer, inkjet, and dye sublimation proofers. The laser thermal transfer proof produces halftone dots with the same screening as will be used for output on plate. The inkjet proof contains ink "spots" that do not have the same screen ruling or angle as those of the printed product. The image from the dye sublimation proofer looks fuzzy due to the imaging mechanism, in which colored dye condenses onto the substrate.

Gray balance. Due to the spectral impurities, process-color inks, when overprinted, tend to produce a pinkish or brownish cast that is most noticeable in neutral gray but affects all colors. Part of assessing the color reproduction requirements, or "fingerprinting," of a press is to determine the relative percentages of cyan, magenta, and yellow required to produce neutral gray.

It is important to check proofs and press sheets for color casts. These can be observed in neutral gray areas of images as well as in gray-balance charts and black versus three-color tone scales.

Color correction. Gray balance (or, more accurately color casts—the lack of gray balance) is an artifact resulting from the spectral impurities of inks that are noticeable when all three inks (cyan, magenta, and yellow) are printed together. Color correction, the need to selectively adjust colors, also results from spectral impurities that are apparent when two inks are printed together.

To assess the color rendition of a proof versus a press sheet, examine the memory colors that are commonly associated with objects. Examine red apples, green grass, and blue sky. Note whether one or more of these colors seem too warm (biased toward the red end of the spectrum) or too cool (toward the blue end). Remember that color casts (gray balance) affect all colors at once, whereas color correction pertains to individual colors. If the flesh tones, grass, and sky all seem too warm, this may be a color cast. If the flesh tones seem too warm and the grass too bluish, while neutral grays are neutral, then this points to the need for color correction.

Density. Solid density (of toner, colorant, or dye) refers to the light-stopping power of color on paper, measured through the complementary-colored filter. When proofing for a printing specification (SWOP, SNAP, PROP, GRACoL), compare the solid densities of the proof with the specified densities and density tolerances in the specification.

Dot gain. Dot gain refers to the apparent increase in dot size from digital file to proof or press sheet. Dot gain is typically greatest at the 50% dot area, which is usually where halftone dots have the greatest perimeter. If it is desired to express dot gain in one number, dot gain at 50% is typically quoted. To get a complete dot gain profile, a tone scale (0–100% dot area, in 10% increments) can be measured. Dot gain can be graphed as percent dot area (file) versus percent dot gain (proof or press sheet). A graph with fewer points can be plotted using 25%, 50%, and 75% tint patches.

Hue error. A number between 0–100%, hue error expresses deviation of a process-color ink from an ideal hue (0% hue error) by comparing reflectances from the two non-complementary colored filters with that of the complementary-colored filter. (For example, to determine the hue error of cyan ink, reflectances through the green and blue filters are compared with that through the red filter.) Hue error for a proof and press sheet should be similar if close color matching is to be achieved. When using a published specification for comparison, refer to the published hue error specification, or measure the hue error of the supplied ink reference, if available.

GATF Color Hexagon. The color hexagon is a densitometric diagram derived from measurements of cyan, magenta, and yellow inks and red, green, and blue overprints. All six colors can be measured from solid patches and from 75%, 50%, and 25% tint patches to form four concentric hexagons. The color hexagon conveys information about tone reproduction, density, and hue error.

The six colors appear as points on the hexagon. Distance from the center corresponds with saturation (density). The axes of the hexagon correspond to ideal ink hues, so deviation from these axes indicates hue error.

COLORIMETRIC EVALUATION

Using a spectrophotometer, ink and proof colorant can be compared in CIELAB, a standardized space corresponding to the gamut of the human eye. In the CIELAB diagram, hues are arranged around the circumference of the circle, while saturation increases from gray in the center to saturated colors on the perimeter. Color differences can be expressed as the distance between two points in CIELAB space, known as Delta E (ΔE).

RIP ONCE, WRITE MANY TIMES

Many potential buyers of digital proofing devices are concerned that problems might occur when one RIP is used to interpret PostScript data for the proofing device, and another RIP interprets the files for the platesetter. This has led many consumers to seek solutions in which a single RIP can drive both the digital proofer and the platesetter. This process is sometimes called "RIP once, write many times," since the RIPed data can be written to a digital blueline plotter, a digital color proofer, and/or a platesetter. Companies offering the RIP-once, write-many-times architecture include Linotype-Hell, RAMPAGE, Scitex, and Screen.

While the potential for two dissimilar RIPs to interpret PostScript data differently cannot be ignored, the number of successful CTP installations without a consistent RIP architecture for proofing and platemaking suggests that these concerns are often exaggerated. In fact, even a prepress department where one RIP drives both the proofing device and the platemaking device is somewhat prone to errors if the PostScript data must be sent to the RIP twice (once at low resolution for the digital proofer, and again at a higher resolution for the platesetter).

5 THE IMAGE CARRIER

The main objective of prepress developments of the last few years has been the elimination of manual operations and intermediate films by the ability to go directly from the original copy to the printing plate. These abilities and constraints have driven platemaking developments in two major directions:
1. High-speed plates exposable by digitally-driven lasers or projection systems
2. Aqueous-based plates to avoid environmental problems

The importance of lasers in forwarding this objective—indeed, their importance in the printing industry overall—cannot be understated. "Light Amplification by Stimulated Emission of Radiation" is the concept of stimulated emission first postulated by Albert Einstein in 1917 where light is produced by atomic processes.

The driving force behind laser plates has been the availability of new light sources and the ability of materials manufacturers to adapt processes in order to take advantage of that availability. As volume usage has grown, prices have tumbled, affording the graphic arts industry a wider and wider choice of sources, at rapidly diminishing prices.

Starting from the original conventional high-powered yttrium-aluminum-garnet (YAG) water-cooled laser the industry has seen the adoption of argon ion (Ar), through to helium-neon (HeNe), frequency-doubled YAG (Fd:YAG), and more recently the availability of solid-state devices such as laser diodes (LD) and light-emitting diodes (LEDs). Lasers are either single beam, using a high-speed rotating mirror to reflect the beam at great speed onto the plate, or are used in an array so that coverage is effectively increased by a factor of 6, 8, or 10, depending on the array format, or a single beam split into 32 arrays, which in turn can be used in parallel to provide coverage.

Imagesetter and plate manufacturers have an increasing range of laser sources to choose from, including Nd:YAG. Operating at 1064 nm in the high-infrared range, Nd:YAG lasers offer a great deal of power, making them suitable for thermal-reacting materials, and especially in the development of infrared (IR) plates. Internal-drum platesetters, for example, use Nd:YAG.

PLATE TECHNOLOGY

One of the key issues concerning CTP technology is the printing plate itself. An important requirement for CTP plates already at their planning stage is that they must be sensitive to certain laser spectral images.

The light-sensitive coating on conventional aluminum printing plates is usually made of diazo. Other possible coatings are photopolymer, inorganic and organic photoconductors, or silver halide.

Materials commonly used as substrates for lithographic plates include aluminum, polyester, and paper. Aluminum has the advantage of being strong and dimensionally stable, but at higher expense. Aluminum plates are used for high-quality, long-run jobs, typically 100,000–1,000,000 copies. Manufacturers offer varying plate thicknesses from 0.008–0.020 in. (0.2–0.5 mm). Polyester is cheaper than aluminum but is not as dimensionally stable, tending to stretch on press, although this is becoming less of a problem. Polyester plates, which use the silver-halide imaging process, are used mostly for black-and-white work, in runs of up to 25,000 impressions. Common thicknesses are 0.004–0.007 in. (0.1–0.18 mm). In recent years manufacturers have improved the stability of polyester and now recommend it for short-run four-color work.

BASIC IMAGING MECHANISMS

Lithographic plates constitute a planographic method of printing, as the image and nonimage areas are distinguished by chemical properties rather than differences in plate surface relief. In conventional (versus waterless) offset plates, the nonimage area consists of aluminum, polyester, or paper treated to accept water, while image areas are composed of compounds that accept oil-based inks. Waterless printing replaces the fountain solution (water) and water-receptive plate surface with a nonstick, ink-repelling surface.

Whether they are manufactured for lamp exposure by vacuum frame or laser exposure in a platesetter, plates are imaged by means of light-sensitive coatings. ("Light" can be interpreted broadly to mean ultraviolet radiation, visible, or infrared radiation.) Depending upon the imaging mechanism, plates can be described as positive-working or negative-working. With a negative-working CTP plate, as with negative-working conventional plates or film, exposure creates the image areas, such as type, line art, or halftone dots. In positive-working plates, exposure creates the nonimage areas, or background. Light from the exposure frame's source is blocked by the black images and transmitted by the clear background.

If the ink-receptive materials are left behind after processing, the plate is termed subtractive. If the image areas are built up on the plate during processing, the plate is additive. Negative plates are generally subtractive.

Platesetter exposure can be set up so that the laser exposes either the image ("write black") or nonimage areas ("write white"). Positive plates are set up to write white; negative plates are set up to write black.

A number of high-speed light-sensitive lithographic plates are available that can be imaged by lasers directly from computerized digital data without the need for intermediate films. These are of six types: plates with silver-halide coatings on film and metal bases; high-speed photopolymer plates with dye-sensitized coatings on aluminum; hybrid plates; thermal-based coatings; inkjet; and electrophotographic plates on an aluminum base.

SILVER HALIDE

Silver-halide plates are very light sensitive and easy to operate, but have so far suffered from lower run lengths. These plates are positive-working plates. They are exposed in "write white" mode on the platesetter, so that the laser writes the nonimage area of the plate. Light-sensitive silver halide (e.g., AgCl) is suspended in the emulsion layer, which lies on top of a positive or "nuclei" layer. The two layers are separated by a "barrier" layer. During exposure of the nonimage areas, laser light catalyzes the reduction of AgCl to molecular silver, which remains in the emulsion layer and does not affect the hydrophilic printing surface. During the first processing step, unexposed AgCl from the emulsion layer diffuses through the barrier layer into the nuclei layer, where it is reduced to molecular silver. During the second processing step, the emulsion layer, barrier layer, and unexposed areas of the nuclei layer are removed. The image areas on the processed plate are formed by oleophilic molecular silver on the plate surface.

Silver halide plate processing involves two stages: an activator and a stabilizer. In the activator stage, a strongly basic solution dissolves the unexposed silver halide in the emulsion layer, after which it diffuses into the positive layer. In the positive layer, centers of development cause silver to precipitate, leaving metallic silver on the plate surface. After the development is complete, the plate enters the stabilizing tank where the weakly acidic solution neutralizes the alkali in the emulsion layer of the plate and stabilizes the precipitated silver.

PHOTOPOLYMER

The disadvantage of photopolymer is that it requires light-sensitive developing solutions that have a tendency to foam. In addition, the plate has to be heated after exposure and yet does not offer the best light sensitivity. On the other hand it has very good run lengths and print characteristics.

Photopolymer plates are negative-working plates exposed in "write black" mode. Photopolymer is a light-sensitive plastic. During processing, unexposed emulsion is dissolved by the developer, leaving exposed photopolymer behind to form the image areas of the plate.

Hybrid

Hybrid plate technology is unique in that it uses two separate and distinct photosensitive coatings on the metal plates. The top coating is a silver-halide emulsion whose light sensitivity can be varied to handle a full range of speeds from contact to film speed and a full gamut of spectral responses from UV to visible blue, green, red, and infrared lasers. The bottom coating is a photopolymer known for good performance on the press. The top coating provides a wide gamut of light sensitivities to accomplish imaging for contact, projection, camera, or CTP printing with controlled dot gain and image contrast. The bottom coating provides ease of printing characteristics that result in high productivity and consistent quality such as plate life, durability, ease of makeready, and maintenance of ink-water balance, ink transfer, register, and other running controls on the press. The advantage claimed for silver-hybrid technology is that the finished plate is indistinguishable from a conventional plate by the time it gets to the press and as a result is immediately accepted by press operators.

The hybrid plate is a combination of silver diffusion and photopolymer plate technologies. It uses a normal silver halide emulsion on top of a photopolymer emulsion, conventional UV-imaged printing plate. The plate is imaged by a low-power argon-ion or YAG laser in the same process as a silver-diffusion plate, creating an image on the top emulsion. Then the plate is processed through two stages. The first stage uses a silver developing process like silver-halide film, but without the clear film substrate. Instead of that, this silver-halide image puts the photopolymer emulsion directly on the top of the printing plate. The second stage is to image the photopolymer emulsion with a standard UV light source, using the silver image as a mask to image the emulsion on the plate conventionally.

These plates share the benefits of the silver diffusion and photopolymer plates, and they can hold a dot range of 1–99%, but run on the press more like a traditional plate with run lengths of up to 300,000 impressions. They have the same environmental limitations as silver-diffusion plates, and the plate processor is larger and more complex. These processors need to be cleaned more frequently than the processors for silver-diffusion or photopolymer plates.

Hybrid plates are positive-working plates that are exposed in "write white" mode on the platesetter. They are made with a combination of silver halide and photopolymer emulsions. The silver halide emulsion, which is very sensitive, enables the plate to be exposed with lower-power laser sources.

Exposure of the silver halide (nonimage areas) causes it to precipitate as molecular silver in the first stage of processing. Black silver forms a mask over the photopolymer layer. A secondary exposure, made inside the processor, hardens the photopolymer exposed through the silver halide mask. Subsequently the silver halide and unexposed photopolymer are dissolved in processing, leaving the insoluble, exposed photopolymer behind to form a positive image.

Thermal

Thermal plates are true digital plates. Once imaged, the dot size conforms to the size of the laser's imaging spot, and it doesn't change if the plate is processed. They can hold very fine dot structures; they are environmentally clean with no chemical processing and can be handled in either yellow safelight or controlled-daylight conditions; and they have the same handling characteristics as conventional presensitized plates.

The thermal plate is the most remarkable technology in printing, but thermal plates cannot be imaged by most of the current generation of platesetters. As their name implies, thermal plates are imaged by heat rather than light. The lasers that are able to image them are very different from the current argon-ion and Fd:YAG lasers. The thermal plate needs higher laser energy to create images than the energy used to image conventional plates.

Most suppliers have created plates sensitive to either 830 nm or 1064 nm or both to satisfy the needs of internal and external drum users.

INKJET

A new approach to CTP is the use of inkjet compounds deposited on grained aluminum. The Polychrome approach uses the inkjet ink to create a mask for light exposure and a processing wash; and the Scitex Iris approach creates a positive image on each of four plates for process-color printing. The Polychrome system has been used by book printers. The Iris system is being configured for small to medium printing firms.

ELECTROPHOTOGRAPHIC PLATES ON METAL BASES

The first of these plates was the Kalle Elfasol plate, used with argon-ion lasers in EOCOM laser platemakers. This and other electrophotographic plates by Howson-Algraphy and Chemco (now Konica) were developed mainly for the newspaper market. The DIC/Polychrome electrophotographic plate uses an organic photoconductor (OPC) and liquid toners to obtain quality suitable for the commercial printing market.

PLATE HANDLING

There are essentially two types of plate-handling systems: manual and automatic. Some suppliers claim a middle ground that they may call "semiautomatic." The difference has to do with the level of human interaction. Our definition of automatic is, very simply, no manual intervention of any kind. After plates are loaded into the device, the device itself removes interleaved paper sheets if there are any, moves the plate to the exposure area, loads it for exposure, exposes it, removes it from the exposure area, and routes it to an on-line processor.

The opposite end of the spectrum would be where a person loads the plate into the exposure area and then removes it after exposure and physically carries it to the processor. Thus, any other approach would be between these two methods. If a person loaded the plate into the exposure area, but the platesetter then exposed it and moved it to the processor, that would be semiautomatic.

Users of CTP systems usually use automatic approaches if they make 50 plates per day or more. Manual users make 50 plates per day or less, but this is not a firm rule.

Handling large vs. small plates. The majority of existing systems at least offer automatic plate loading equipment, which is seen as imperative from the large customer's point of view to avoid damaging the plate. Automatic plate handling systems add to the cost of CTP, and in order to make the entry-level cost more attractive to a larger number of printers, a number of suppliers are offering defeatured, manual loading systems. If you are intending to expose smaller plates, B3 (13.90×19.68 in.) or less, you may want to consider the manual loading option. Also, be aware that the future thermal plates can be handled in daylight, which could make the need for automatic handling redundant.

Slip sheets. Automatic systems must deal with slip sheets. All of them have developed approaches that sense the difference between the slip sheet and the aluminum plate, and thus can deal with the sheet and then select the plate. Automatic plate handling contributes to overall productivity. Plates supplied come with interleaved paper sheets between each plate. Some platesetters take plate boxes as supplied, slit them open at one end, and load them directly into the machine. They then take the plates from the box one by one, and remove the interleaf sheet automatically. Other suppliers require the customer to take plates from the delivery boxes and load them into cassettes. In some cases the interleaving sheets have to be removed manually.

Punching. There is still debate over whether to punch the plate before or after exposure. It cannot be done in the platesetter because of the delicacy of the optics. Companies advocating pre-punching refer to the time and difficulty of achieving accurate register by post-punching, but our discussions with manufacturers would not support those reservations, normal post-punching taking only a matter of 15–20 seconds to achieve register.

PLATESETTERS

The platesetter function is to guide a precisely focused laser beam across a fairly large area, and to lay down overlapping laser dots. The time taken to carry this out is referred to as exposure time, which should be as short as possible.

Your selection of a platesetter will depend upon the size of plates you want to expose using CTP, but generally speaking, the larger the format and the higher the resolution required, the more money it is going to cost. We can categorize systems as:

- 66×82-in. very large format
- 55×67-in. large format
- 41×52-in. format
- 32×42-in. format
- 22×28-in. format

Platesetters image plates with different lasers. Recent trends suggest that the 830- and 1064-nm lasers may dominate because of their use with new thermal plates. The plates that are imaged employ three technologies: silver diffusion, silver mask (or hybrid), and photopolymer.

Some systems directly image conventional presensitized plates, providing a benefit of cost savings in using conventional plates as compared to their digital counterparts. Standard presensitized plates require a high-power UV light source where they are flood exposed. Using these plates with a digital platesetter is impossible since each pixel on the plate (a 28×40-in. plate at a resolution of

2000 dpi supports 4.48×10^9 pixels in total) would need to be exposed for literally hours.

CTP TECHNOLOGY: DRY TONER TRANSFER

The secret to the recent rejuvenation of the small offset press as a viable alternative to the high-speed copier and the digital-press markets can be attributed to a new CTP process geared toward the high-growth, short-run, small offset market. CTP technology permits the transfer of electronic data directly to a printing plate. Until recently, the small offset market was not able to take advantage of the benefits and efficiencies CTP has to offer due to the sizable investment in the hardware required. Entry level to CTP technology ranged from $30,000 to $500,000 for systems that produce laser-imaged metal plates (run lengths to one million), laser-ablation transfer (LAT) technology, and a special version of a silver-based photo-direct plate that can be imaged in an imagesetter.

A new type of technology has emerged to address the burdens and torments of the small offset market and provide the answer for an extremely low entry cost for CTP. The new plate technology can be classified under a new category called dry toner transfer (DTT), which means that the plate is simply imaged from the "dry" toner of a properly designed laser printer/platemaker. A properly designed laser printer/platemaker for DTT offers:

- High resolution
- Large format to handle press-size plates
- 4–8 pages per minute (PPM), the slower the engine the more fusing time for toner to bake into the plates
- Minimal toner scatter

DTT derives its name from the fact that the toner particles from a laser printer are transferred directly onto the surface of the plate. The coating of the DTT plate has hydrophilic properties (water loving), and the surface of the plate is designed and manufactured to simulate grooves and the rough surface of a metal plate, allowing retention of water for as long as possible. While the hydrophilic coating and the texture of the plate accepts the water and rejects the ink, it is the actual toner particles of the image (fused onto the plate by a properly designed laser printer) that effectively attract and hold the ink.

Applications for this technology include printing business cards, invitations, announcements, newsletters, mailer coupons, tabs, stationery, imprinting (holiday cards, calendars, checks, pads), sales literature, flyers, catalog sheets, labels, certificates, etc. This technology can also be used by in-plant departments and larger commercial print shops that have small duplicator presses for most of their short-run requirements.

Unlike electrostatic plates or laser plates that use electrostatic technology, this new generation of laser-printer-to-plate does not require a hazardous conversion (etching) solution to activate it. In fact, no plate conversion is necessary at all. DTT plates work as soon as they are output from the laser printer; they can be immediately mounted onto press. Electrostatic plates act as their own photoreceptor that requires further processing, whereas DTT plates utilize the simplicity and efficiency of the laser printer's photoreceptive drum to transfer the image to its surface, requiring no further activation or processing.

The DTT plate system offers several major advantages and benefits to the small offset market. It has the lowest CTP entry investment, i.e., the price of a properly designed laser printer, which can also be utilized for other applications such as proofing, creating camera-ready art and copy, etc. Production costs are lower, since many costly consumables are eliminated from the process and the cost per plate is lower. Production turnaround time is faster as more than four steps are eliminated from the traditional platemaking process.

The potential customer base is increased since electronic files can be accepted and output. DTT technology competes in the "on-demand," "just-in-time," and "distribute-then-print" arenas, and gives the small offset press a position as a viable technology for digital commerce. New file transfer techniques (via internet or modem software) allow the small offset printer to receive files and be press-ready in moments.

KEY ELEMENTS FOR OPTIMAL DTT RESULTS

Laser printer size and resolution. DTT plates should be imaged in a newer A3 (12×18-in.) laser printer. The larger-format laser printers usually have higher resolution and would allow output large enough for most duplicator or small web press plate sizes. The laser printer resolution should be at least 1200×1200 dpi to provide a line ruling of 100 lpi with 65 gray levels, or an 1800×1800-dpi printer to provide 196 gray levels at a screen ruling of 100 lpi. A DTT plate will provide an image equal to the output quality of the laser printer.

Toner scatter. Toner scatter occurs with most laser printers. If the toner particles are not removed from the nonimage area, a slight toning will appear during the pressrun as the toner begins to pick up ink. The simple remedy to eliminate the unwanted toner scatter is in a new breed of environmentally friendly "plate cleaner" products that are commercially available. Simply wipe the entire surface of the plate with the "cleaner" in small circular motions and the top layer of toner scatter is effectively removed, allowing for clean and crisp reproductions on press.

Fusing temperature. The toner must be properly fused (baked) to the plate to assure long pressruns. Most laser printers have inadequate fusing temperatures for optimal results with DTT plates. The laser printer used should offer four to eight pages per minute. Laser printers that offer faster throughput normally do not allow for proper fusing of DTT plates. When optimal fusing is accomplished, the plates can offer run lengths exceeding 20,000 impressions. If the toner is not properly fused/baked onto the surface of the plate, the image can begin to break off very early in the pressrun. Several laser printer manufacturers are providing platemaker laser printers designed with the proper fusing temperature and minimal toner scatter conditions to flawlessly output the plates.

If a laser printer was recently purchased, but does not fit the requirements or specifications to properly output a DTT plate, a low-cost "off-line" external fuser/baking unit can be purchased that would allow for the proper fusing temperature of the plates.

Decontamination of the press and striving for a pH balance of 4.5–5.5. Since no plates are as forgiving or as water-loving as metal, DTT plates are more sensitive to contaminants in the press. If the pH balance is not within the window of 4.5–5.5, there is a greater chance of toning in the nonimage area. If the scattered toner particles have been removed from the background of the plate (with plate cleaner) and toning occurs during the pressrun, it is normally attributed to the pH of the fountain solution being too high or too low.

Not only does the new DTT technology offer the local print shop the least expensive, most efficient, and environmentally friendly way to go direct-to-plate, but the actual cost per plate is typically half the price of a metal plate and competitive with photo-direct plates. With the new breed of plates there are no more expenditures for hazardous processing chemistry, masking materials, films, or etches. In addition, because the plates are "toner activated," they are not light-sensitive and therefore have an unlimited shelf life. The new DTT plate technology has effectively renewed the life of the investment of the small offset press, and has spawned a new era of digital commerce for the small local printer who can finally compete in the short-run "on-demand" revolution.

Even if a small print shop decides not to switch to this technology now, it may be a good idea to keep at least a couple of boxes of the plates in storage just in case a processor, camera, or operator is down for a period of time. Using the proper laser printer and the new generation of DTT plates, a shop can be back in business and press-ready with a click of the mouse.

6 QUALITY CONTROL

Quality control simply refers to the steps taken to ensure the production of a quality printed piece that meets the expectations of the end user or customer. There are various techniques, methods, and devices to help verify quality, including inspection, testing, customer service, batch sampling, and calibrating instruments used to measure quality.

PLATESETTER CALIBRATION

The GATF/Systems of Merritt Digital Plate Control Target is a test device written in native PostScript language. It is designed to monitor electronic imaging devices, particularly platesetters and imagesetters. The digital file displays data obtained directly from the raster image processor (RIP). It contains a variety of targets sensitive to exposure, resolution, and directional effects. The physical dimensions of the imaged target are 0.5×6.0 in. (12.7×152.4 mm).

This target has been developed in response to the increasing use of digital workflows where it is often inconvenient and/or impractical to resort to traditional film-based targets to monitor process variations. The Digital Plate Control Target provides an easy-to-use tool for confirming that input specifications are being observed by an electronic imaging device and that the output is at a consistent level of quality. It eliminates the uncertainty about whether the RIP in an electronic imaging device is following the operator's instructions or being diverted by internal or external overrides, and whether it is capable of performing as requested. It provides a consistent means of monitoring exposure level, checking imaging resolution, diagnosing directional effects or image inconsistencies, and confirming platesetter/imagesetter linearization.

When the Digital Plate Control Target is used in accordance with the procedures set forth in the user's guide it will provide valuable feedback as to whether an electronic imaging device is performing within specifications and with a high degree of consistency. Specifically, the target can tell whether the requested resolution is being utilized for output, how well the imaging device writes in horizontal versus vertical directions, whether data with circular or semi-circular components is rendered with fidelity equal to horizontal and vertical elements, whether the addressability of the imaging device is sufficient to render the requested level of fine detail, whether areas of solid coverage have sufficient maximum density (D_{max}) values, and how well requested halftone dot percentages are rendered on output.

The GATF/Systems of Merritt Digital Plate Control Target is best analyzed with a combination of visual and measurement techniques. Several of the crucial elements are evaluated with the aid of a hand magnifier, while the tone scales are best quantified with reflection or optical measurements. Studies have shown that measurements on printing plates can be effective if the measuring devices are properly tested and calibrated with the particular plate being used.

The information block should be examined to determine if the output of the RIP is the same frequency, angle, and spot function as was specified in prepress. (The Digital Plate Control Target recognizes the frequency, angle, and spot function override feature of Harlequin RIPs.) When the target images a small dagger shape beside one of these values, it indicates that the RIP has overridden the value specified in the application program. The value accompanying the dagger will be the actual value on the plate, not the specified value from the application.

After imaging the Digital Plate Control Target onto a plate or film, the elements of the target can be analyzed according to the following steps: horizontal and vertical microlines; one-pixel through four-pixel checkerboard; negative and positive curved microlines; star target; solid patch; 50/150 and 50/200 reference tints; and uncorrected and corrected tone scales.

CALIBRATING CTP PLATES

CTP plates generally can be calibrated using the PostScript transfer function on the platesetter's RIP, meaning that dot sizes on plate can be adjusted and controlled relatively precisely. Dot sizes on plate can be read relatively accurately using a new type of plate-reading densitometer that uses a CCD array to accurately differentiate the image from nonimage areas of the plate and thereby reads the geometric dot area on plate. Current examples include the Acme Platereader and BetaScreen CCDot. There are three approaches to determining the dot values that plates should have:

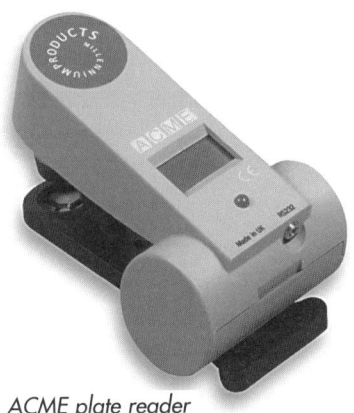

ACME plate reader

1. Linear. This approach seeks to calibrate the platesetter so that the dot size requested in digital files is accurate on plate—e.g., a 50% dot in a file actually measures 50% on the plate. There are two problems with this approach.

The first problem is that exposure of conventional plates in a vacuum frame adds about 2–6% dot gain to the plates, so linear CTP plates will not match conventional plates on press. For example, the 50% dot on a conventional plate may actually be 55%, while that on a linearized CTP plate will be 50%. The 5% difference in plate gain will be apparent on press as lighter reproductions with the CTP plate.

The second problem is that the dot gain specifications of SWOP, SNAP, and GRACoL were based on conventional plates with their inherent plate gain. So, even if no conventional plates are used in the plant, linear CTP plates cannot come up to the dot gain specified by today's printing specifications, as they print too "sharp" or light.

2. Calibrated to analog. This approach is used when a plant is running both conventional and CTP plates. This may occur when some work requires film and other work is totally digital, or when the firm is making a transition from conventional to CTP plates. As mentioned before, conventional, vacuum frame-exposed plates have inherent dot gain on the plate, due to light undercutting the dots on the negative plate. The calibrated-to-analog approach aims to optimize exposure of plates in the vacuum frame using a plate exposure target such as the GATF Plate Control Target or UGRA Plate Control Wedge. Such targets provide halftone dots and continuous-tone step wedges to verify optimal plate exposure. Using the tone scale, dot gain can be read throughout the tone reproduction scale, e.g., at 10, 20, 30, . . . , 90% dot area. The plate gain on the optimized analog plate is then used as a specification to which the platesetter is calibrated. This approach theoretically produces CTP plates that match analog plates on press. However, even if an analog and digital plate read the same dot sizes with a plate-reading densitometer, images on the two plates may not match exactly because the ink/water balance characteristics of the plate may differ. Therefore, successful calibration of digital to analog plates needs to be done with reference to a printed test form, in which the dot sizes on press sheets are compared both visually and densitometrically.

3. Optimized for print specification. The third approach is to include a "virtual" plate gain curve in the CTP plate so that printing can achieve the dot gain throughout the tone scale that is specified in a national printing specification. Such a curve may include, for example, a 5% gain at the midtone and gradually diminish to less gain in the highlights and shadows. The difference between the optimized and analog approaches is that the dot gain curve on an analog plate may not be smooth or symmetrical from the highlights to the shadows.

THE NEED FOR CALIBRATION

CTP is only productive if the end result can be accurately predicted. Since all the components use different physical properties to carry out their functions, and many of these can only be determined subjectively, it is crucial that, where possible, the most important parameters correspond. This is particularly true for color calibration.

Newly installed monitors, scanners, proofers, RIPs, and plate recorders all have their own system parameters. Calibration is therefore the process of adjusting each component so that at each point in the production line the same input data produces the same output data.

COLOR MANAGEMENT

Like the well-known instant rice, the most successful process color reproductions in CTP jobs will be those that come out right "the first time, every time." Advantages of computer-to-plate technology, including reduction in labor and turnaround time, are achieved from the ability to record images directly from digital files onto printing plates.

CTP workflow short circuits opportunities for marking up off-press proofs and rescanning, retouching, and/or dot etching to achieve color changes traditionally associated with high-quality critical color or commercial color work. "Chasing color" is incompatible with CTP workflow because final imaging is done directly on the plate.

Color management is an important tool in achieving accurate color reproduction.

COLOR REPRODUCTION AND COLOR MATCHING

Recognizing the inherent quality differences between color transparency film versus process-color ink on paper, it is important to distinguish between color "reproduction" and color "matching." Consider a 4×5-in. transparency that is separated for reproduction on uncoated paper. The color-reproduction medium of the transparency consists of cyan, magenta, and yellow dyes with truer hues and higher densities than those of ink on paper. While the transparency may be able to reproduce perhaps a 10,000-color gamut, the process-color inks on uncoated paper can reproduce perhaps 3,000 colors. To "match" the transparency's reproduction on press is an unrealistic expectation, and ignores the great differences in quality and cost between the two media. What we really want, and can reasonably hope to achieve, is an optimal reproduction on press.

CLOSED-LOOP AND OPEN-SYSTEM COLOR

There are two useful approaches to color reproduction: "closed-loop color," in which color reproduction characteristics are determined by test target analysis and settings are manually entered into the scanning or image-editing software; and "open-system color," in which a color management software program is used to derive and make color settings.

The premise of closed-loop color is that if scanner adjustments for separations and halftones are based on press characteristics, then reproduction will be optimized. Closed-loop color could be defined as the analysis of four- (or more-) color printing characteristics, through the use of test targets that are analyzed visually and/or with color measurement instruments, to determine prepress settings required for optimum color reproduction ("matching"). Determining press characteristics to make scanner settings, and making these settings on the scanner, "closes the loop" between scanner and press, but only for those two devices.

Color management uses device-independent color space as a connection between input and output devices, and could be termed open-system color. This is useful when the color "loop" cannot be "closed" because (1) the user does not know at the time of scanning what output device will be used, (2) multiple output devices will be used, and/or (3) the user cannot afford the time and effort in learning the analytical procedures necessary to implement closed-loop color.

Color management attempts to make color more predictable. It translates color between devices using a device-independent profile connection space and standard profiles for each device that characterize its color reproduction capabilities. Color transformation is performed by a color management module (CMM). By using a profile for each device and a CMM, applications can offer a wide range of features that can reduce the time and cost of reproducing color. These include:
- More accurate reproduction between devices
- Use of the display as a proofing device, known as soft proofing
- Device simulation, or the ability to simulate one device on another for the purpose of proofing
- Gamut checking and mapping, which can determine if a particular color can be reproduced on a particular device, and if not, selecting the closest color that can be reproduced
- Profile embedding, which allows users to store profiles that contain information about the device in images and other color objects.

THE "THREE Cs" OF COLOR MANAGEMENT

Many people use the term "calibration" to mean all steps necessary to achieve accurate color during the production process, perhaps implying that reproduced colors are "calibrated" to match the original. "Color management" is a more meaningful term for matching color on different input and output devices, since the calibration of each device is only the first of three steps necessary to achieve accurate and consistent color throughout the reproduction process.

Calibration ensures that all devices (scanner, monitor, and printer) perform to a known specification, be it RGB illuminance, CMYK density, or CMYK dot area.

Characterization is a way of measuring and quantifying the color space, color gamut, or color behavior of a particular device under known conditions. It is a way of determining how an input device captures color or an output device records color when it is calibrated.

Conversion (also known as color transformation or color correction) refers to translating a color image from the color space of one device to that of another under known conditions. Color conversion can be done by manually correcting the image or automatically by using color management software.

To achieve the goals of color management, calibration, characterization, and conversion must be done in this sequence. Calibrating a device to specification serves as a foundation for characterization and conversion, and a device must be characterized before color data can be converted for accurate rendering.

CALIBRATION

Color management is based on the assurance that all devices in a color reproduction system are performing to specification. Calibration alone does not guarantee color matching; it simply ensures that the scanner, monitor, and printer are performing to their respective specifications, and provides a way of ensuring they will be consistent over time.

Scanner calibration means that when a specific light level is measured from a film or paper target, the scanner consistently records a corresponding digital value in the image file for that spot on the original. Monitor calibration means that the display card consistently displays a pixel corresponding to the specific digital value received from the file. Other items that require calibration include the color printer/proofer and the platesetter.

CHARACTERIZATION

After devices are calibrated, they must be characterized. Characterization defines the color gamut, or set of reproducible colors, that an input device can capture or an output device can record. Device characterizations are stored as profiles, digital files of data describing the color gamut of a device. In page-layout software, color management systems keep track of the input, display, and output devices the user has specified using tags or data appended to color files.

A variety of models can be used to characterize input and output devices, including RGB color space, CMYK color space, and CIE color space, which includes two models based on the dimensions of hue, chroma, and value. These are the CIExyY and CIELAB color spaces. In both models, hues are arranged around the perimeter of the color space, saturation increases from center to edge, and value varies along the third color space axis.

Scanners are characterized by software that measures the values in a scanned IT8.7 target and compares them to corresponding values in a reference file. The IT8.7 target is the internationally standard input target developed by the IT8 subcommittee of the Committee for Graphic Arts Technologies Standards. The basis of the IT8.7 target is the Q60, a series of photographic film and paper test images for characterizing the gamut of input devices developed by the Eastman Kodak Co.

The printer must also be characterized. Output targets are measured with a spectrophotometer in CIExyY and/or CIELAB color space to characterize the color gamut of an output device. As with scanners, the characterizations are stored as device profiles.

Profiles for commonly available monitors are offered by the developers of color management software, although they are valid only when the monitor is performing to manufacturer's specifications. Some software allows users to characterize their own monitors; other systems have built-in calibration.

CONVERSION

Conversion refers to translating color-image data from the color space of one device to that of another under known conditions. Color conversion is necessary so that a scanned image reproduces as a believable representation of the original on both the screen and the printer. Since output devices typically have smaller color gamuts than originals, scanners, and monitors, colors in the original must be fit into the gamut of the device, a process known as gamut compression.

Color management software converts or translates color from one space to another: from scanner to monitor, from monitor to printer, and from scanner to printer.

Once color management profiling software has been used to characterize the scanner, monitor, and printer, it is necessary to apply the profiles to the image according to the desired "matching" objectives.

Three methods of color conversion are used—one for photographs, one for spot colors, and another for business graphics. *Perceptual rendering*, used for continuous-tone photographs, maintains the relative range of colors in a photograph. It causes the white portions of an image to have no ink on the paper, and the black portions to have the darkest color that the device can print.

Colorimetric rendering, most effective for spot colors, maintains an absolute color match. It renders colors that are within the device's gamut identically, and brings colors outside the gamut to the closest color the device can print.

Saturation rendering is appropriate for bright saturated illustrations and graphs like those used in business presentations. This rendering style produces pure, saturated colors in print according to the printing device's limitations. It does not try to precisely match printed colors to those on the monitor.

COLOR MEASUREMENT DEVICES

Four types of colorimeters or spectrophotometers can generally be used with color management programs:

Manual. This refers to instruments in which each patch is measured by hand. Manual measurement is practical for infrequent measurement of profiling targets that contain about 200 or fewer color patches. Depending upon the instrument used, manual measurement of 200 patches takes about a half hour.

x-scanning. To alleviate some of the drudgery of measuring patches, instruments that scan in one direction, such as certain colorimeters and spectrophotometers, can automatically read color targets in strips and transmit the measurements to the computer. Since these instruments scan in one dimension only, they are referred to as x-scanning instruments. Strip-reading instruments considerably speed up the process of reading color patches over manual reading, but may require specially formatted targets and a higher level of user knowledge.

x/y-scanning. Further automation is provided by x/y-scanning instruments, which scan in two dimensions (x and y), Depending on the model and cost, x/y-scanning instruments may be faster or slower than x-scanning instruments.

Calibrated scanner. Some programs enable output device characterization targets to be read with a calibrated scanner. In this case the scanner is used as an x/y-scanning colorimeter.

CONVENTIONAL COLOR MANAGEMENT

Conventional color management, sometimes known as "fingerprinting" the press or determining its color reproduction requirements, refers to the printing and analysis of test images to determine the optimum color reproduction settings for halftones and color separations. Settings derived from such analysis are implemented in scanning/image-editing software.

Conventional color management requires more time and expertise to implement than automatic color management, but it may be useful in situations where:

- The user does not have, or does not want to invest in, color management hardware/software, including a color-managed scanning program, monitor calibration/characterization instruments and software, and output calibration/characterization instruments and software

- Scanning and output are done in-house, where managers have both control over the image-reproduction process, from scanning through output, and the expertise to determine optimum color reproduction settings
- Scans are generally reproduced under the same printing conditions, including press, paper, and ink, so that, once determined, color reproduction settings change very little, if at all.

Conventional color reproduction requirements include tone reproduction, referring to image contrast; gray balance, the process of determining the proper balance of cyan, magenta, and yellow inks to reproduce neutral gray, hence eliminating color casts; and color correction, the process of achieving accurate hue and realistic color saturation.

TONE REPRODUCTION

Tone reproduction refers to image contrast, including lightness and darkness.

Settings. Tone reproduction settings include the picture highlight, shadow, and midtone. To make tone reproduction settings on a scanned image, the operator must know in advance the minimum printing dot, maximum printing dot, and midtone dot gain on press. Knowing this information provides three easy-to-make settings that significantly improve raw scans and, when working without automatic color management, frees desktop scanner operators from depending upon unreliable on-screen appearance for making image adjustments.

Highlight and shadow. The highlight dot, or minimum printing dot, and shadow dot, or maximum printing dot, determine the contrast range available for reproducing an image with ink on paper. Thus, the highlights and shadows are important in optimizing the lightness and darkness of black-and-white halftones and color separations. Optimal highlight and shadow dot sizes are determined by printing a test target called a highlight/shadow patch, which is included in GATF digital test forms, and can also be easily constructed in page-layout or drawing software. The highlight/shadow patch contains a series of highlight and shadow dots with ranges anticipated to encompass the minimum and maximum dot, respectively, on papers, inks, and presses to be tested (e.g., highlight dots from 0–10% dot area, shadow dots from 80–100% dot area).

After printing the highlight and shadow patch, the user examines the target with a magnifier to determine the smallest and largest dots, respectively, that are reproduced. Highlight dots below the minimum printing dot "blow out," or fail to image, leaving white paper. Shadow dots above the maximum print dot "fill in" as solid ink.

Midtone. The midtone refers to the density, or gray level, of the original at which the midtone, or 50% dot, reproduces. (Referring to the midtone as 50% dots means that the percent dot area of these dots measures 50% on film or plate, from a calibrated imagesetter or platesetter. After dot gain on press, the midtone would be equal to the 50% dots on plate, for example, plus the net gain in apparent dot area on paper.)

Dot gain (more specifically, total or apparent dot gain) on press results from physical ink spread and absorption into the paper (physical dot gain) and from the dot "shadow," or blocked reflectance of light underneath the dot, on translucent substrates (optical dot gain). Dot gain is measured with a densitometer and expressed as the net (not percentage) increase in apparent dot area of dots, from digital file to substrate. As an example, if 50% dots in a digital image file measure 70% after printing on paper, the dot gain is 20%.

The everyday user need not be concerned with separating total dot gain into physical and optical gain. These two components can, however, be quantified by comparing the physical dot gain, measured with the GATF Dot Gain Scale© II, with the total dot gain, measured densitometrically.

Dot gain can be compensated by adjusting the midtone of scanned images. The midtone of an image is quantified as the density range between the highlight and midtone. For example, if the midtone is placed at a density of 1.20 and the highlight at 0.30, the highlight-to-midtone range is 0.90.

The operator should include a 12-step grayscale alongside the photograph to set the midtone accurately and consistently. The midtone can then be set by placing the 50% dots on a specified grayscale step (e.g., step 5, 6, or 7 of a 12-step scale), according to the amount of dot gain anticipated and the desired lightness/darkness of the reproduction. If a grayscale has not been included with the scan, the operator can set the midtone by referring to the image appearance on screen, but accurate screen appearance requires screen calibration, which is part of automatic color management.

Gray balance. Gray balance is the adjustment of cyan, magenta, and yellow (CMY) dot sizes to produce a neutral gray. Because of the spectral impurities of process inks, overprinting equal percentages of each color tends to form a pinkish brown color rather than gray or black. Throughout a reproduction, these impurities can cause a color cast. By finding out what percentages of CMY are required to produce neutral gray, the separator can reproduce all colors accurately.

In lithography, gray balance is influenced by many materials and press variables, including the hues of process color inks, quality and color of paper surface, ink film thickness printed on paper, ink trapping, printing sequence, press printing characteristics, and dot gain. Recognizing the complexity of attaining gray balance, GATF offered a test image in 1969 for determining gray balance requirements for a particular combination of ink, paper, and press. A similar chart, the Tone Reproduction and Neutral Determination System (TRAND), was introduced in 1972 by the Technical and Education Center at Rochester Institute of Technology. Both charts consist of patches of varying yellow and magenta tint percentages at different tone values. Each tone level consists of a matrix of tint patches, with varying magenta values in rows and varying yellow values in columns. The cyan dot size is constant for all squares in a given matrix.

After the chart is printed on a press operating within normal production control limits, the most neutral patch in each matrix of squares is located. For visual evaluation, a photographic or printed halftone grayscale can be used as a reference for comparison under standard viewing conditions. Punching holes in the grayscale makes it easier to compare with the patches. If a grayscale or standard viewing conditions are not available, the target can be evaluated with a color reflection densitometer to find the patch in each matrix with equal red, green, and blue filter densities. For more accurate instrument readings, a colorimeter may be used to identify the patch that measures the closest to the paper in CIELAB color space, that is, with a* (red-green) and b* (blue-yellow) values closest to those of the paper, to which the eye adapts as neutral white.

Color correction. Original colors can be changed during the separation process. This is useful for three reasons: to print the best reproduction regardless of the substrate and inks used; to optimize the reproduction of different original film emulsions; and to change colors according to customer preference. Color correction is accomplished by the adjustment of cyan, magenta, yellow, and black (CMYK) printers with respect to specific original colors. "Color Correction Theory & Techniques," *GATF SecondSight* 15, reviews this topic.

Color correction for commercially-available process inks is necessary because they are impure and absorb some of the light that they should transmit. No process ink has the ideal characteristic of one-third spectral absorption and two-thirds spectral transmittance.

These spectral impurities are quantified as hue error, a number between zero and 100% (zero meaning a pure color, 100% meaning an incorrect color). Without color correction, reds have an orange cast and blues have a purple cast. To counteract ink hue error, color correction can be used to adjust the hue and saturation of printed colors to be more accurate.

Once color correction is set up to compensate for ink hue error, it can be further refined for accurate reproduction of different dyes in photographic materials.

The third use of color correction is to change the colors in a separation to suit the customer's preference. Customers may want specific colors to appear more or less saturated or to have a different hue. Such changes can be accomplished with selective color correction.

UCR/GCR. Removing equal amounts of yellow, magenta, and cyan process color inks from shadows and replacing them with a corresponding amount of black ink began with the introduction of undercolor removal (UCR) with photographic separations. A related process, gray component replacement (GCR), involves removing colors from gray areas throughout the reproduction. Both processes are termed *achromatic color reduction.*

UCR helps to save ink, shorten drying time, and avoid setoff or ink transfer to the bottom of press sheets in a stack. GCR adds further ink savings and improves color stability on press, but also reduces the ability to change color on press by adjusting ink density.

Achromatic color reduction can be specified in two ways: as a percentage from 1–100% (e.g., 50% GCR) or as total ink coverage (assuming that solid four-color process inks would total 400% coverage). SWOP specifications for magazines call for a maximum total ink coverage less than 300%, while SNAP specifications for newsprint allow 240%. Desktop color software usually features UCR and GCR, which can be set as total ink coverage.

7 Workflow

In discussing workflow for CTP applications, it is useful to compare and contrast traditional and digital workflow, as in the models presented on the following pages. These models do not necessarily encompass all traditional or digital workflow options, but are presented as typical examples.

Traditional workflow. The model of traditional workflow includes many steps, often performed in separate departments using different equipment operated by specialized craftspersons.

A typical design concept in the traditional model begins with small-scale thumbnail sketches, progressing to a full-scale rough layout leading to a detailed, comprehensive design mockup. Text for the job is set using dedicated typesetting equipment, leading to a galley proof for proofreading and pasteup. Pasteup copy is termed a page proof.

Black-and-white and color photography is done on a 35-mm, medium-format, or view camera. Exposures on medium-format and view cameras are verified using a special filmback for Polaroid film, and exposures are bracketed to help ensure that a picture is produced with the correct exposure.

The art board serves as a place for collecting and organizing the page content. Line work is subject to line art photography, while halftones and color separations are done on the process camera or on an electronic color scanner that outputs film or loose scans. Color separations are checked using an overlay or laminated proofing system. If corrections are needed, these are done by rescanning or through the process of dot etching.

Traditional Workflow

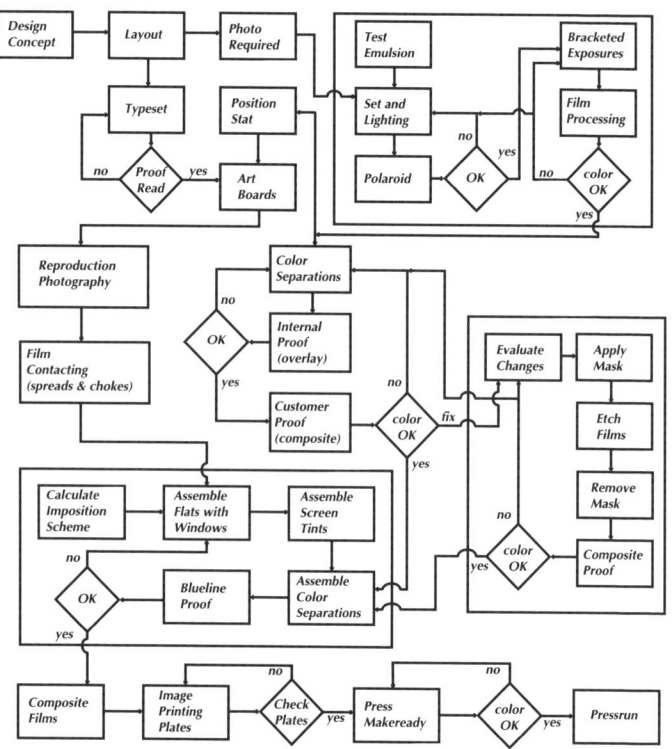

Once satisfactory line art, halftone, and color separation films are produced, they are manually assembled into flats for imposition. At this stage, screen tints are applied, if needed, and a blueline proof is made to check imposition and to provide a final content check. Composite film flats are then used to image printing plates.

Digital workflow. The model of digital workflow stresses the condensation of production steps and their migration from printers, or service providers, to publishers, authors, photographers, and other content providers.

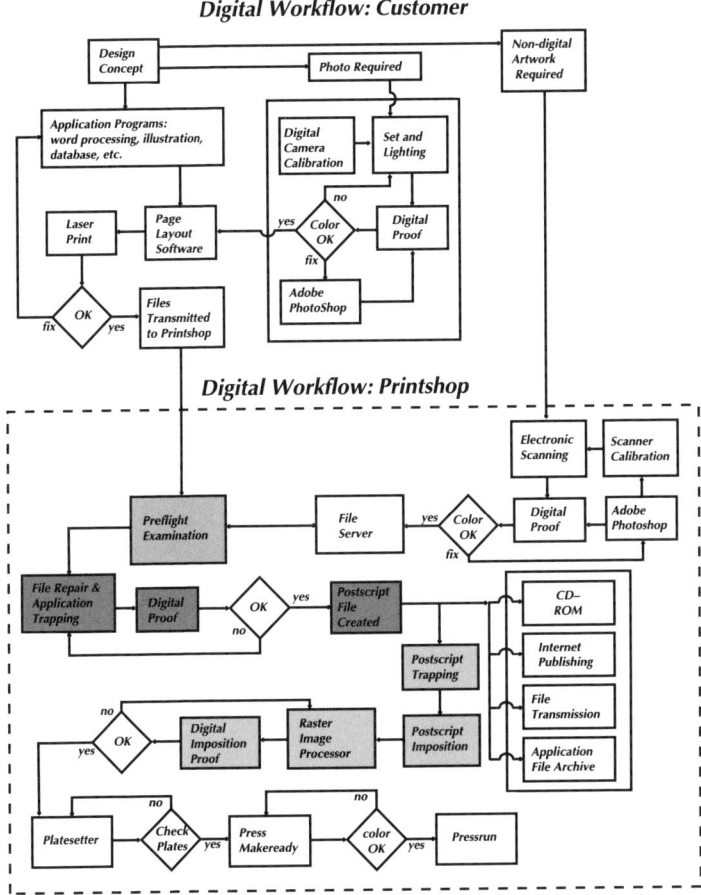

Digital, like traditional, production begins with a design concept. In digital workflow, however, the design of type and graphics may be initiated in a word processing, illustration, spreadsheet, database, or other computer program. Pages are created using page-layout software, and type and position are checked on a black-and-white laser printer.

If a photo is required, it may be acquired via a digital camera. Prior to exposing the photo, the photographer will set up the set

GATF's 12-Step Plan for Adopting a CTP Workflow

1. Identify your objectives and set your goals. Do your homework by comparing the features and prices of the available CTP systems, and calculating the return on investment for the devices you are interested in. Make sure CTP is the appropriate response to your needs. If you have workflow problems that CTP won't fix, address them first!

2. Implement quality control and color management procedures throughout your scanning, color correction, proofing, output, and press areas. Examine the tools already in place for measuring and controlling quality, and make any necessary improvements.

3. Become proficient at preflighting all your files to catch mistakes before they are output.

4. Learn to do all your trapping electronically. Acquire trapping software if necessary.

5. Become comfortable with outputting imposed film using imposition software.

6. Acquire an electronic proofing system for full-color page proofs. Build customer confidence by continuing to output random scans to film with photomechanical proofs. During the transition, show both types of proofs to your customer. Use a spectrophotometer and proof-checking software to maintain quality and consistency of all your proofs.

7. Upgrade your network to at least 10BaseT, and preferably to 100BaseTX.

8. Install an image server with queue management and OPI functions. Consider one with color management capabilities.

9. Upgrade your archiving procedures, and make sure that you have the means to archive terabytes of data.

10. Buy a CTP platesetter and RIP. Start by imaging fully imposed film, and continue to use photomechanical proofing during the steepest part of the learning curve.

11. At the same time, buy a roll-fed wide inkjet plotter for imposed proofs (a digital blueline) unless your CTP platesetter can also generate inexpensive imposition proofs.

12. Analyze the effectiveness of your digital workflow. Look for unanticipated problems that require monitoring, identification, and resolution. Once you've overcome these issues, remove the film, and enjoy the savings!

and lighting, then make a digital proof to check the content and exposure. If the color is acceptable, the digital photo can be incorporated into the page layout by saving it in a standard image file format. If the color needs to be changed, options include taking another photo or doing color correction in an image-editing program like Adobe Photoshop. Photos from transparencies, prints, or negatives can also be included in artwork. To do so, content providers will generally use flatbed scanners, dedicated slide scanners, and/or desktop drum scanners.

If the content provider needs or prefers to have scans made, photos will be sent to the service provider for scanning, generally on a desktop drum or high-end drum scanner. The service provider will need to calibrate the scanner for optimum tone and color reproduction on the output device prior to making the scan, and will check the quality of the color using a digital proof. If color changes are needed, the photos can be rescanned or changes can be made with image-editing software. Once the color is acceptable, the images will be stored on a file server.

On receiving page layout files from the content provider, the service provider will likely subject the files to a preflight examination to make sure all elements (fonts, linked graphics, colors, and settings) are included and set properly. If file repair and application trapping are necessary, these will be done prior to imaging a digital page proof. If the proof is okay, a PostScript file can be created. Optionally, imposition and trapping can be done on the PostScript file, before or after it is RIPed. An imposition proof can be used to check the imposition. Once okay, the file can be transmitted to the platesetter. Alternative uses of files include CD-ROM, Internet, transmission of the file to another service provider, and archival storage.

Digital workflow includes many process steps, most of which can be automated.

8 Return on Investment

The installation of any new technology is based on a tangible benefit to the company, a return on the investment (ROI). In the past we have experienced significant returns because of savings in personnel, consumables, or waste. CTP savings come down to:

- **Media**. The elimination of film, its chemistry, and its disposal. But CTP plates may be priced higher than conventional plates, thus reducing the potential savings.
- **Labor**. The elimination of manual stripping and plate-handling labor, but this may be lessened if you have to add new digital workers, or already lessened through new digital prepress operations.
- **Proofing**. You cut time and labor for analog proofing, but the cost per proof may be slightly higher, depending on your need to see "dots."
- **Turnaround time**. You can make changes faster and do more jobs because the press is no longer waiting for plates. CTP systems are making at least eight eight-up plates per hour at about 1200 dpi.
- **Waste**. The accuracy and repeatability of CTP reduce waste due to fewer makeovers required because of variability in the process of plate exposure from film.
- **Makeready**. Substantial savings on press are being recorded, from 10 to 25%. New digital plates are cleaner on press and register faster. Dots are harder and sharper and placed more precisely.

Early users of computer-to-plate systems report that much of the ROI in CTP is in the pressroom. Good color on press is the result of a sequence of factors that go from the press (paper, press condition, ink and water balance) to platemaking (dot gain, registration, processor chemistry) and back to film (dot gain, registration, processor chemistry). A good plate must hold fine detail and be accurately exposed and processed. All the plates in a set must register. If a plate isn't perfect on all counts, makeready time and waste go up, and quality is compromised. Thus, if we can make plates more consistently, we can get on press and on paper faster.

The steps in conventional platemaking are well known. Film is exposed in an imagesetter and processed. Variation in film sensitivity, exposure, laser power, and processing all affect dot gain and color. Manual stripping of film can result in misregistration. Contact exposure is another opportunity for misregistration, and another set of process variables (plate sensitivity, exposure time, and processing) that affect dot gain.

The platemaking environment is also a problem. A 20°F change in temperature could cause a 40-in. aluminum plate to change size by 1.5 dot-rows at 150 lpi, a visible registration error. A smaller shift may appear to be in register when you align the film, but color will vary across the press sheet. Film also changes size—a 10% change in humidity will cause a dot-row change in a 40-in. 150-lpi film. Making or remaking a plate in an uncontrolled environment is asking for problems in the pressroom. Many platerooms do not have this level of variability, but some may.

CTP makes the road to printing more consistent by removing steps. Variation in film exposure, film processing, and film fit, as well as misregistration on the stripping table and in the contact frame are eliminated. The plate should have better-formed dots since it is a first-generation product. Plate quality from even the best platesetter may be limited by variations in plate sensitivity, platesetter exposure, and plate processing.

With thermal plates the coating responds to light that becomes heat and must be raised above a threshold temperature where the plate is exposed and nothing more happens. Below the threshold, the plate remains unexposed. A light-sensitive plate remembers how much exposure it has been given and can be fogged, underexposed, or overexposed. Thermal plates are insensitive to process variation, giving remarkably consistent results.

Some CTP manufacturers may image thermal plates with a Gaussian spot—a spot that is bright in the middle and dim at the edges. The longer the exposure to a Gaussian spot, the larger the pixel imaged on the plate, even on a thermal plate. Any variation in power level, exposure time, or dust on the platesetter optics changes the resulting spot size and defeats the consistency of the thermal material. But most CTP users are using photopolymer and hybrid plates. They are very happy with the quality results and have immediate ROIs. The plates are cheaper than thermal, the process steps are cut, the variability is reduced, and the savings in the pressroom are enough to matter.

To evaluate an investment in CTP, you must quantify equipment investments and take into account future changes—software upgrades, maintenance over time, etc. Ascertain from plate suppliers the actual cost of the CTP plates they will supply. The plate decision is probably the first decision you should make. Analyze workflow changes that CTP will require, including employee changes. You will reduce labor requirements in stripping but will also require certain specialized CTP-related personnel.

It may be that for the immediate future, a film impositing or hybrid route, involving "digitization" of your company operation and outputting to film or polyester plate, may make economic sense in the short term.

The economies of going CTP will depend upon the prices you are going to be asked to pay. Some suppliers are talking about a 20% or more premium for their CTP plates, which in many cases will make the investment barely worthwhile.

IS CTP FOR YOU?

Rapid changes are taking place in telecommunications and the trend to digital origination by customers. CTP can represent an opportunity to increase productivity while consolidating your business. It will increase your productivity through savings in materials and labor costs, while offering the chance to tie in customers through the management of their databases.

If you want CTP, look at your business as it is today, and how you expect it to change over the next three years. Evaluate the following:

- The type of orders your company deals with, in terms of quality. Generally speaking, the higher the print quality produced by your company, the higher the demands that are placed on the CTP prepress system.
- The quantity of orders, per year, broken down by:
  — process color work
  — spot color
  — black-and-white
- The volume throughput of each expressed as number of pages per year
- The volume and quality of proofing required
- Which types of orders are handled best
- Which types of orders cause problems, either because they are too complex and don't fit in with the natural workflow, or they are too complex to be handled economically by existing resources
- How much of your present origination is already available in digital format
- How likely to change are your customers

Because CTP requires a reorganization of existing work practices, investment is going to involve redeployment and retraining. While CTP offers savings in personnel employed in conventional tasks, it requires the training and development of a new breed of operator who is computer-literate. If there are personnel within the company who can be trained, it will cost money or new people will have to be brought in. We have heard that CTP involves de-skilling the workforce, but we see otherwise. CTP requires knowledge of the following—digital typesetting, digital imposition, digital color management, digital proofing, color trapping for the specified press, and digital workflow—all of which ultimately needs to be in-house expertise and this will involve retraining the workforce.

Elements of ROI

The following is a short list of things to consider when determining an ROI for a CTP investment.

Plate usage. Calculate annual plate consumption of the work that will be transferred to CTP, broken down by square footage. A waste factor of 5% should be allowed for. Silver-based and photopolymer plates cost less than thermal plates.

Film usage. It takes about 1.25 square feet of film for each page, or a total of 10 square feet for the eight-up plate. Film costs also vary widely, depending on volume and competition. The savings in film is negated by the premium for the digital plate. Now, if the printing company is paying to dispose of the film and chemistry and is also reaping some benefit from silver recovery, the net cost could be more.

Personnel. Quantify the number of personnel employed in the conventional function, by job, and the annual wage bill. CTP certainly reduces stripping and platemaking labor. However, prepress automation in the last few years has already cut much of that labor. Plus, there will be the need for CTP personnel to load plates, set up imposition and jobs, and output proofs. The net personnel savings depend on the size of the "manual" operation. As a rule of thumb, we have found most firms that have implemented CTP to have saved at least 2.5 full-time employees. We must note that some saved more and some did not save any. Every firm retrained personnel for other jobs within the plant. (Saving half a person is an interesting personnel management challenge.)

Space. The CTP system and associated processor require about 50% of the space that a stripping, analog proofing, and platemaking facility does. Square footage rates also vary widely. (Be prepared to maintain the conventional system for a year or so as you make the transition to CTP.)

Investment. We have seen plants that amortized the CTP system over as few as three years and as many as ten years. Five years tends to be the average. And every early CTP investor is prepared for 5–10% reinvestment every year, for upgrades and improvements. (Include an element in the CTP cost of the potential interest that could be earned from the capital investment if that money was not spent on CTP.)

Maintenance. Use 12% of the total of all hardware and software for maintenance. This is an annual requirement.

Other costs. The platesetter is only the tip of the iceberg. You will also need digital proofing (color and black-and-white), high-capacity storage for work in process and archiving, and high-speed networking. These "infrastructure" costs could be as high as the CTP investment if the plant has not already implemented many of them as a part of digital prepress.

THE BOTTOM LINE

To be competitive with alternative methods for information dissemination, printing will have to produce extremely high-quality images with extremely short turnaround. CTP will increase quality and cut time—in the latter case, by as much as half. Early adopters have found that they must look at every aspect of operation within the plant to provide a new level of ROI that goes beyond traditional methodologies.

Glossary of Terms

Achromatic Without color or hue (black and white).

Adobe Acrobat A popular portable document file (PDF) format. Through Acrobat or another PDF, users can read electronic versions of printed documents that maintain the attributes assigned to a printed original. See also *portable document format.*

Aluminum plate A thin sheet of specially grained aluminum used as a lithographic image carrier.

Analog device A computer or other device that uses continuous signals of varying intensity rather than digital signals that can only be "on" or "off."

Array A group of light-sensitive recording elements often arranged in a line. Used as a scanner image-sensing device.

ASCII file A text file containing no special formatting.

Banding An electronic prepress term referring to visible steps in shades of a gradient.

Bandwidth A frequency measurement expressed in cycles per second (hertz) or bits per second (bps) of the amount of information that can flow through a channel.

Batch processing Automated execution of a set of instructions on a sequence of computer files.

Bimetal plate A lithographic printing plate made from two metals, one forming the ink-receptive image area (usually copper) and one forming the water-receptive nonimage area (chromium, stainless steel, aluminum, zinc, etc.).

Binary code A representation of information using a sequence of zeros and ones. See *bit* and *byte.*

Bit The smallest unit of information used in a computer file. It has one of two possible values—zero or one—used to indicate "on" or "off," "yes" or "no" in the storage and transfer of electronic information and images. See *byte.*

Bitmap An image represented by an array of picture elements, each of which is encoded as a single binary digit. See *line images, raster, vectors.*

Blanket A rubber-coated fabric mounted on a cylinder that receives the inked impression from the plate and transfers (or offsets) it to the paper.

Blanket cylinder The cylinder that carries the offset rubber blanket, placing it in contact with the inked image on the plate cylinder and then transferring the inked image to the paper carried by the impression cylinder. The blanket cylinder has a gap where the blanket clamps are located. The outer ends of the cylinder house the bearers.

Bleed (1) A printing area that extends to the edge of the sheet or page after it is trimmed. (2) A slight extension or thickening of printing detail, usually of the lighter color or tint, to produce color overlap zones, so that a white gap will not show in printing when slight variations in register occur.

BLUELINE   A blue-on-white print made by exposing sensitized paper to a negative in contact. It is used as a final proof before platemaking.

BYTE   A single group of bits (most often eight) that are processed as a unit. Also the smallest addressable unit of main storage in a computer system. See *bit*.

CALIBRATION   A process by which a scanner, monitor, or output device is adjusted to provide a more accurate display and reproduction of image.

CAMERA, DIGITAL   A photographic system using a charged-coupled device (CCD) to transform visual information into pixels that are assigned binary codes so that they can be manipulated, compressed, stored, or transmitted as electronic files.

CCD ARRAY   A group of light-sensitive recording elements often arranged in a line (linear array) and used as a scanner image-sensing device. See *charge-coupled device*.

CEPS   Abbreviation for *color electronic prepress system*.

CHARGE-COUPLED DEVICE   A component of an electronic scanner that digitizes images. A CCD consists of a set of image-sensing elements (photosites) arranged in a linear or area array. Images are digitized by an external light source that illuminates the source document, which reflects the light through optics onto the silicon light sensors in the array. This generates electrical signals in each photosite proportional to the intensity of the illumination.

CIE L*A*B   Scales adopted by the International Commission on Illumination (CIE) to serve as a worldwide standard for color measurement.

CMYK   Abbreviation for *cyan, magenta, yellow*, and *key* (black), the four process colors or inks. The letters are occasionally rearranged to indicate a specific printing sequence.

COLOR BALANCE   (1) The correct combination of cyan, magenta, and yellow needed to reproduce a specific photograph without an unwanted color cast or color bias. (2) The specific combination of yellow, magenta, and cyan needed to produce a neutral gray in the color separation process. (3) The ability of a film to reproduce the colors in an original scene. Color films are balanced during manufacture to compensate for exposure to specific light sources.

COLOR CAST   Modifying a hue by adding a trace of another hue to create such combinations as yellowish green or pinkish blue. Color casts can be undesirable as in the contamination of the desired hue by the second hue.

COLOR CONVERSION   Producing a color transparency from a color reflection original so that a flexible copy of the original can be color-separated on a rotary-drum scanner.

COLOR CORRECTION   A photographic, electronic, or manual procedure used to compensate for the deficiencies of the process inks and color separation.

COLOR GAMUT   The range of colors that can be formed by all possible combinations of the colorants in a color reproduction system.

COLOR MANAGEMENT SYSTEM   An electronic prepress tool that provides a way to correlate the color-rendering capabilities of input devices (scanners and digital cameras), color monitors, and output devices (digital color proofers, imagesetters, color printers) to produce predictable, consistent color. Color management consists of three steps: (1) calibration of input devices, monitors, and output devices to known specifications, (2) characterization, which is a way of determining the color "profile" of a particular device, and (3) conversion, which performs the "color correction" function between color-imaging devices.

COLOR MATCH Condition resulting when no significant difference in hue, saturation, and lightness can be detected between two color samples viewed under standard illumination.

COLOR PATCH Small samples of the inks that will be used for a process-color job. They are printed on the required paper stock and attached to the original art to serve as a reference in the color separation process.

COLOR REPRODUCTION GUIDE A test image containing examples of solid primary colors, secondary colors, three- and four-color images, and tint areas that serves as the standard for correcting defects in printing ink pigments and the color separation process.

COLOR SCANNER A device incorporating a digital or analog computer that separates colored originals electronically by using the three additive primary colors of light in the form of blue, green, and red filters, plus a pre-programmed black printer correctly balanced with the color separations. A light beam moves over the image point by point, generating a separate, color-corrected, continuous-tone intermediate or screened halftone film negative or positive representing each of the process colors and black.

COLOR SEPARATION Using red, green, and blue filters to divide the colors of a multicolored original into the three process colors and black. The four resulting film intermediates are used to prepare the yellow, magenta, cyan, and black printing plates. Color separation is most often accomplished with an electronic color scanner.

COLOR SPACE The three-dimensional area where three color attributes, such as hue, value, and chroma, can be depicted, calculated, and charted.

COLORIMETER An instrument that measures and compares the hue, purity, and brightness of colors in a manner that simulates how people perceive color.

COMPRESSION Reducing the size of a file for storage purposes or to enhance the speed of data transfer by eliminating the redundancies and other unnecessary elements from the original.

COMPUTER GRAPHICS Producing graphic material from computer systems. This process often involves integrating text and art and completing page layout on the computer before outputting it to a laser printer or imagesetter.

CONTINUOUS TONE A photographic image or art that has not been screened. It has infinite tone gradations between the lightest highlights and the deepest shadows.

CONTINUOUS-TONE GRAYSCALE A scale of uniform tones, from white to black or transparent to opaque, without a visible texture or dot formation.

CONTINUOUS-TONE NEGATIVE An inverse impression of tones from the original reproduced on sensitized film without using a visible texture or dot formation.

CONTINUOUS-TONE PROOF An illustration without halftone dots, which is produced on a computer screen at view file or fine file resolutions with the red, green, blue color separations.

COPYDOT TECHNIQUE Photographing halftone illustrations and associated line copy without rescreening the illustration. The halftone dots of the original are copied as line material.

CREEP (1) Movement of the blanket surface or plate packing caused by static conditions or by the squeezing action that occurs during image transfer. (2) The displacement of each page location in the layout of a book signature as a result of folding the press sheet.

CREF Abbreviation for *computer-ready electronic file.*

CYAN A blue-green color, complementary to red. One of the three primary subtractive, or process, colors used in the printing process.

CYLINDER A roller with grippers that hold and press the sheet against the inked form roller on a printing press.

DARKROOM The light-tight chamber in which photographic materials are handled and processed.

DATA Text, audio, video, and images stored in a form that can be understood by a computer.

DATA CONVERSION Technique of changing digital information from its original code so that it can be recorded by an electronic device using a different code.

DATABASE An electronic program that is used to efficiently organize, store, retrieve, and modify information, such as a mailing list.

DENSITOMETER An instrument for measuring the optical density of a negative or positive transparency, or of a print.

DENSITY (1) The light-stopping ability of an image or base material, sometimes referred to as optical density. (2) A photographic term used to describe the tonal value of an area. (3) The specific gravity or weight per unit volume of paper.

DESKTOP PUBLISHING The creation of fully composed pages with all text and graphics in place on a system that includes a personal computer with a color monitor, word processing, page makeup, illustration, and other off-the-shelf software; digitized type fonts; a laser printer; and other peripherals, such as an optical image scanner.

DIGITAL Method of representing information in numerical (binary) code.

DIRECT DIGITAL COLOR PROOF (DDCP) Proof printed directly from computer data to paper or another substrate without creating separation films first.

DIRECT-TO-PLATE TECHNOLOGY Those imaging systems that receive fully paginated materials electronically from computers and expose this information to plates in platesetters or imagesetters without creating film intermediates.

DOT The individual element of a halftone. It may be square, elliptical, or a variety of other shapes.

DOT GAIN The optical increase in the size of a halftone dot during prepress operations or the mechanical increase in halftone dot size that occurs as the image is transferred from plate to blanket to paper.

DOWNLOAD To transfer a file or files from a remote computer to a local computer's hard drive.

DOWNTIME The period of time in which a device is not working because the system is malfunctioning or maintenance is being performed.

Drum A synonym for cylinder.

Drum scanner Color separation equipment on which the original transparency is wrapped around a hollow, plastic rotary cylinder.

EPS (1) Encapsulated PostScript. (2) Electronic printing systems.

Exposure The period of time during which a light-sensitive surface is subjected to the action of actinic light.

File transfer protocol (FTP) The tool used to retrieve information in the form of electronic files from any number of computer systems linked via the TCP/IP protocol. Users in effect transfer copies of information found on remote computers either directly to their own computers or to a service provider's network and then to their own computers.

Film Sheets of flexible translucent or transparent acetate, vinyl, or other plastic base materials that are coated with a photographic emulsion.

Flat A sheet of film or goldenrod paper to which negatives or positives have been attached (stripped) for exposure as a unit onto a printing plate.

Flexography One of the major printing processes. Employs a flexible rubber or photopolymer plate that has the image areas in relief (i.e., raised) above the nonimage areas. Used primarily to print products for the packaging industry.

Fog A photographic defect in which the image is either locally or entirely veiled by a deposit of silver. Caused by stray light or improperly compounded chemical solutions.

Four-color process printing The photomechanical reproduction of multicolor images achieved by overprinting specified amounts and areas of yellow, magenta, cyan, and black inks.

Full bleed An image extending to all four edges of the press sheet, leaving no visible margins.

Galley (1) The raw output of a phototypesetter, usually in the form of single columns of type on long sheets of photographic paper, which serve as preliminary proofs. (2) The final typeset or imageset copy output to photographic paper, or directly to film.

Gamut The greatest possible range.

Gigabit (Gb) One billion bits.

Gigabyte (GB) One thousand megabytes or one billion bytes.

Graphic communications Allied industries, including printing, publishing, advertising, and design, that participate in the production and dissemination of text and images by printed or electronic means.

Graphics interchange format (GIF) Originally developed specifically for compressing photographic images online, GIF is the most common method of encoding and storing picture files on the World Wide Web.

Gravure A printing process that uses an image carrier in which the image is engraved or etched below the nonimage surface. The image carrier is coated with ink, with the excess ink being scraped off. The inked image is transferred to paper or another substrate by contact.

Gray balance The values for yellow, magenta, and cyan that produce a neutral gray with no dominant hue when printed at a normal density.

Gray component replacement (GCR) An electronic color scanning capability in which the least dominant process color is replaced with an appropriate value of black in areas where yellow, magenta, and cyan overprint.

GRAYSCALE A reflection or transmission film strip showing neutral tones in a range of graduated steps. Exposed along with originals during photography, it is used to time development, determine color balance, or measure density range, tone reproduction, and print contrast.

GRIPPERS The metal clamps or fingers located on impression cylinders and transfer cylinders that grasp and hold a sheet while being transported through the press.

HALFTONE Tone values represented by a series of evenly spaced dots of varying size and shape, the dot areas varying in direct proportion to the intensity of the tones they represent.

HIGHLIGHT The lightest or whitest area of an original or reproduction, and represented by the densest portion of a continuous-tone negative and by the smallest dot formation on a halftone and image carrier.

HUE A visual property determined by the dominant light wavelengths reflected or transmitted.

HUE ERROR A measure of the hue deviation from a theoretically perfect subtractive process (primary) color.

HYPERTEXT MARKUP LANGUAGE (HTML) The hypertext document format used on the World Wide Web.

HYPERTEXT TRANSFER PROTOCOL (HTTP) The Internet standard supporting the exchange of information on the World Wide Web.

IMAGE (1) Any picture, drawing, subject, or reproduction visible to the human eye that portrays the original in the proper form, color, and perspective. (2) A picture formed by light. The optical counterpart of an original focused or projected in a photographic camera.

IMAGE AREA On a lithographic printing plate, the area that has been specially treated to receive ink and repel water.

IMAGE CARRIER The device on a printing press that carries an inked image either to an intermediate rubber blanket or directly to the paper or other printing substrate.

IMAGESETTER A device used to output fully paginated text and graphic images at a high resolution onto photographic film, paper, or plates.

IMPOSITION Assembling the various units of a page before printing and placing them on a form so they will fold correctly.

INKJET PRINTING A nonimpact printing process in which a stream of electrostatically charged microscopic ink droplets are projected onto a substrate at a high velocity from a pressurized system.

INK/WATER BALANCE The appropriate amounts of ink and water required to ink the image areas of the plate and keep the nonimage areas clean.

INTERFACE The electronic device that enables one kind of equipment to communicate with or control another.

INTERNET The official name for an international network of computer networks linked to provide and share information and resources.

JOINT PHOTOGRAPHIC EXPERTS GROUP (JPEG) The compression scheme that is a defacto standard on the Internet. Allows the user to control the compression ratio and reproduction quality at the point of compression.

LASER   A high-energy, coherent (single-wavelength) light source. The small spot of light produced by the laser makes it possible to expose light-sensitive and photoconductive materials at high speed and high resolution.

LASER PRINTER   A nonimpact output device that fuses toner to paper to create near-typeset quality text and graphics.

LASER SCANNER   A device that uses color filters, electronic circuitry, and beams of light to produce tone- and color-corrected separations from color originals mounted on rotating drums.

LIGHT SENSITIVE   A material that is chemically altered after it is exposed to light.

LIGHT-EMITTING DIODE (LED)   A small electronic component used on some alphanumeric display panels.

LINE IMAGES   Solid areas with no shading or tones, including type, drawings, and diagrams.

LITHOGRAPHY   A method of printing from a plane surface (a smooth stone or metal plate) on which the image to be printed is ink-receptive and the non-image area ink-repellent.

LOCAL-AREA NETWORK (LAN)   A group of interconnected computers that allow several people at the same business site to access the same set of documents.

LOSSLESS ALGORITHM   A mathematical formula for image compression that assumes that the likely value of a pixel can be inferred from the values of surrounding pixels. Because lossless compression algorithms do not discard any of the data, the decompressed image is identical to the original.

LOSSY ALGORITHM   A mathematical formula for image compression in which the data in an image that is least perceptible to the eye is removed. This improves the speed of data transfer but causes a slight degradation in the decompressed image.

LZW   Abbreviation for *Lempel-Ziv-Welch*, a type of lossless algorithm used for data compression. Compacts image files such as those saved in TIFF and GIF file formats and reduces them them to binary code, which can later be used to reconstruct the file.

MAGENTA   The subtractive transparent primary color that should reflect blue and red and absorb green light.

MAKEREADY   All of the operations necessary to get the press ready to print a job.

MAPPING   Converting encoded data from one format to another, particularly in database management.

MEGABIT   One million bits.

MEGABYTE   One million bytes.

MEMORY   The area in an electronic device where binary-coded information is stored.

MICROLINES   Resolution elements used in the graphic arts to ensure the optimum exposure of photomechanical materials.

MIDTONE DOT   A point in a middle-gray area of a halftone. Its area equals or approaches the average of the nearby background areas.

MIDTONES   The range of tonal values between halftone highlight and shadow areas.

MISREGISTER   Printed images that are incorrectly positioned, either in reference to each other or to the sheet's edges.

MODEM The interface, or communications link, between one computer workstation and another, or a network of computers. A modem converts digital information into analog signals suitable for transfer over telephone lines.

MOIRÉ An undesirable, unintended interference pattern caused by the out-of-register overlap of two or more regular patterns such as dots or lines.

MONITOR SCREEN A cathode-ray tube or liquid crystal display device on which image information is displayed in conjunction with a workstation.

NEGATIVE A photographic film or plate that is exposed and processed to provide a reversed image of the tones found on the original—highlights and shadows or color values.

NEGATIVE-WORKING PLATE A printing plate that is exposed through a film negative. The plate areas exposed to light become the image areas.

NETWORK Essentially, any interconnection of separate components (such as computers), each station of which is capable of transmitting some form of information to another station.

NONIMAGE AREA The portion of a lithographic printing plate that is treated to accept water and repel ink when the plate is on press.

OEM Abbreviation for *original equipment manufacturer*.

ONE-UP Printing a single image once on a press sheet.

ONLINE The state of a computer being connected to and communicating with another electronic device for the purpose of distributing or retrieving information.

OPEN PREPRESS INTERFACE (OPI) A set of standardized protocols that allows desktop equipment to be linked with color electronic prepress systems (CEPS).

OUTPUT DEVICE The machine that translates the electrical impulses representing data as processed by a computer into permanent results. A laser printer, imagesetter, or phototypesetter are some examples.

OVEREXPOSURE A condition in which too much actinic light reaches the film, producing a dense negative or a washed-out print or slide.

OVERPRINT (1) A color made by printing any two of the process inks on top of one another to form red, green, and blue secondary colors. (2) In lithographic platemaking, exposing a second negative onto an area of the plate previously exposed to a different negative. This is a method of combining line and halftone images on the plate. (3) Solid or tint quality control image elements that are printed over or on top of previously printed colors. Used to measure trapping, saturation, and overprint color densities.

PAGE LAYOUT A dummy indicating page size; trimmed job size; top, outside, and foot trims; untrimmed page size; and head, foot, outside, and bind margins.

PAGINATION The process of page makeup.

PANTONE MATCHING SYSTEM (PMS) The most commonly used ink-mixing and color-reference formula.

PHOTOGRAPHIC PROOFS Blue, brown, or silver prints made from negatives or positives and used to check layout and imposition before plates are produced.

Photomechanical All processes in which printing surfaces are produced with the aid of photography.

Photopolymer Plate A relief printing plate made of light-sensitive flexible plastic and most often used in flexography.

PICT A file format for Macintosh-based vector and bitmapped images, used primarily for clipboard images and screen captures.

Pixel Picture element. The smallest tonal element in a digital imaging or display system.

Pixelization A technique used to represent areas of complex detail as relatively large square or rectangular blocks of discrete, uniform colors or tones.

Plate A thin metal, plastic, or paper sheet that serves as the image carrier in many printing processes.

Plate Cylinder The cylinder that holds the printing plate tightly and in register on press. It places the plate in contact with the dampening rollers that wet the nonimage area and the inking rollers that ink the image area, then transfers the inked image to the blanket, which is held on its own cylinder.

Platemaking Preparing a printing plate or other image carrier from a film or flat, including sensitizing the surface if the plate was not presensitized by the manufacturer, exposing it through the flat, and developing or processing and finishing it so that it is ready for the press.

Portable Document Format (PDF) A computer file format that preserves a printed or electronic document's original layout, type fonts, and graphics as one unit for electronic transfer and viewing.

Positive-Working Plate An image carrier that is exposed through a film positive. Plate areas exposed to light become the nonimage areas because they are soluble in the presence of developing agents.

PostScript™ Adobe Systems Inc. tradename for a page description language that enables imagesetters developed by different companies to interpret electronic files from any number of personal computers and off-the-shelf software programs.

PostScript, Encapsulated A file format used to transfer PostScript image information from one program to another.

Preflighting An orderly procedure using a checklist to verify that all components of an electronic file are present and correct prior to submitting the document for high-resolution output.

Prepress All printing operations prior to presswork, including page design and layout, typesetting, graphic arts photography, image assembly, and platemaking.

Pressrun (1) The total of acceptable copies from a single printing. (2) Operating the press during actual job.

Process Colors The three subtractive primary colors used in photomechanical printing (cyan, magenta, and yellow, plus black).

Processor An automatic device that feeds exposed photosensitive paper or film over rollers through baths to develop and dry them before they reach the delivery area.

Proof A prototype of the printed job made photomechanically from a plate (a press proof), photochemically from film and dyes, or digitally from electronic data (prepress proofs).

Proof, soft An intangible, unstable image, such as that on a video screen.

Proofing Producing simulated versions of the final reproduction from films and dyes or digitized data or producing trial images directly from the plate.

Punch A die used in finishing operations to perforate holes or slots in paper or board for looseleaf or mechanical binding or other applications, such as mounting.

Quality control The day-to-day operational techniques and activities that are used to fulfill requirements for quality, such as intermediate and final product inspections, testing incoming materials, and calibrating instruments used to verify product quality.

Random-access memory (RAM) A solid-state computer memory in which the time required to access data is independent of the data location. RAM is the main memory of a microcomputer.

Raster An image composed of a set of horizontal scan lines that are formed sequentially by writing each line following the previous line, particularly on a television screen or computer monitor.

Raster image processor (RIP) The device that interprets all of the page layout information for the marking engine of the imagesetter. PostScript or another page description language serves as an interface between the page layout workstation and the RIP.

Rasterization The process of converting mathematical and digital information into a series of dots for the production of negative or positive film or printing plates.

Reflectance The ratio between the amount of light reflected from a given tone area and the amount of light reflected from a white area.

Register The overall agreement in the position of printing detail on a press sheet, especially the alignment of two or more overprinted colors in multicolor presswork. Register may be observed by agreement of overprinted register marks on a press sheet. In stripping, film flats are usually punched and held together with pins to ensure register. The punched holes on the film flat match those on the plate and press specified for the job.

Register Marks Small reference patterns, guides, or crosses placed on originals before reproduction to aid in color separation and positioning negatives for stripping. Register marks are also used to aid in color register and correct alignment of overprinted colors during printing.

Reproduction Duplicating an original by any photographic or photomechanical process.

Resolution The precision with which an optical, photographic, or photo-mechanical system can render visual image detail. Resolution is a measure of image sharpness or the performance of an optical system.

RGB Abbreviation for *red, green,* and *blue,* the three additive color primaries.

RLE Abbreviation for *run length encoding,* a type of data compression that reduces the size of image files by counting the occurrence of identical pixels in an image and saving merely that count. See *lossless algorithm.*

RTF Abbreviation for *rich text format.*

Saturation The degree to which a chromatic color differs from a gray of the same brightness.

Scan The sequential examination or exposure of a character or pictorial image with a moving light beam.

Scanner (1) An electronic device that uses a light beam to examine color transparencies and isolate each process color on an individual piece of film, or photographic separation, to be used in the reproduction process. (2) Flatbed electronic devices that are used in conjunction with desktop publishing systems to scan line art, logos, photographs, and typewritten or printed text supplied by the client.

Screening The process of converting a continuous-tone photograph to a matrix of dots in sizes proportional to the highlights and shadows of the continuous-tone image.

Server A device on a computer network that allows networked users access to a specific service on the Internet.

Shadow The darkest portion(s) of a print or an original. In halftones, shadows have the largest dots.

Sheetwise Imposition A printing layout in which separate plates (and film flats) are used to print the front and the back of a single press sheet. Completely different pages appear on each side of the sheet.

Signature One or more printed sheets folded to form a multiple page section of a book or pamphlet.

Silver Halide A silver salt suspended in gelatin to prepare the emulsion of photographic film.

Slip Sheet (1) A sheet of paper placed between two freshly printed sheets to prevent setoff or blocking. (2) A protective covering for sensitized plate surfaces.

Snap Abbreviation for *Specifications for Nonheatset Advertising Printing*. A set of standards for color separations and proofing developed for those printing with uncoated paper and newsprint stock.

Spectrophotometer An instrument used to measure the relative intensity of radiation throughout the spectrum as reflected or transmitted by a sample.

Spot Color Printing The selective addition of a nonprocess color ink to a printing job.

Squeeze Printing pressure between the plate and blanket cylinders.

Stochastic Screening A halftoning method that creates the illusion of tones by varying the number (frequency) of micro-sized dots (spots) in a small area. The placement of each spot is determined as a result of a complex algorithm that statistically evaluates and distributes spots under a fixed set of parameters.

Storage Any device—including computer memory and disks— in which data can be stored and accessed or retrieved at a later time.

Stripping The act of combining and positioning all of the copy elements from all of the film negatives or positives together as a negative for platemaking. Also known as *image assembly*. See *imposition*.

Substrate Any base material that can be printed or coated.

Swop Abbreviation for *Specifications for Web Offset Publications*. A set of standards for color separation films and color proofing developed for those involved in publications printing.

Tagged image file format (TIFF) A file format for exchanging bitmapped images (usually scans) between applications.

Telecommunications The transmission of data and/or voice over the network of telephone lines.

Tone The degree of lightness or darkness in any given area of print.

Tone reproduction A comparison of the density of every tone in a reproduction to the corresponding densities on the original.

Transmission control protocol/Internet protocol (TCP/IP) The system that monitors and performs data transfer over the Internet. TCP sends data and IP receives it.

Trapping (1) Printing a wet ink over a previously printed dry or wet ink film. (2) How well one color overlaps another without leaving a white space between the two or generating a third color.

Trim The excess area of a printed form or page in which instructions, register marks, and quality control devices are printed. The trim is cut off before binding.

Two-up Printing two identical pages on the same press sheet, usually by exposing the plate twice to the same negative.

Typeface Name of particular standardized form of type.

Ultraviolet radiation The range of electromagnetic radiation that lies outside the visible spectrum. In the graphic arts, UV rays are used to induce photochemical reactions.

Undercolor removal (UCR) A technique used to reduce the yellow, magenta, and cyan dot percentages in neutral tones by replacing them with increased amounts of black ink.

Underexposure A condition in which too little actinic light reaches a photosensitive paper, plate, or film, producing a thin negative, a dark slide, or a muddy-looking print that lacks detail.

Uniform resource locator (URL) The World Wide Web address of a company, service, or other information resource.

Unix The computer environment in which the Internet has been and continues to be developed. It is used to run powerful workstations and networks where multitasking and multiuser access is essential.

Upload To transmit a file from a local computer's hard drive to the hard drive of a remote computer.

Vectors Mathematical descriptions of images and their placement. In electronic publishing, vector graphics information is transferred from a design workstation to a raster image processor (RIP) that interprets all of the page layout information for the marking engine of the imagesetter. PostScript, or another page description language, serves as an interface between the page layout workstation and the RIP.

Wavelength The distance between corresponding points on two successive waves of light or sound.

Web offset A lithographic printing process in which a press prints on a continuous roll of paper instead of individual sheets.

Work-and-tumble An imposition in which the front and back of a form is printed from a single plate. After the first run through the press, the stock pile is inverted so that the back edge becomes the gripper edge for the second printing.

WORK-AND-TURN A common printing imposition in which all of the images on both sides of a press sheet are placed in such a way that when the sheet is turned over and the gripper edge is used, one-half of the sheet automatically backs up the previously printed half. When the sheet is cut in half parallel to the guide edge, two identical sheets are produced.

WORK-AND-TWIST A method of imposition in which a film flat produces two different images on a plate. After the first exposure, the flat is rotated 180° to produce the second exposure.

WORLD WIDE WEB (WWW) A hypertext program that allows users to access related documents across global networks by navigating a series of electronic links.

WYSIWYG Abbreviation for *what you see is what you get.* Computer screen displays that approximate the true size and true shape of typographic characters, rules, tints, and graphics.

X-COORDINATE The horizontal location of data on a graph, computer monitor, or page layout.

Y-COORDINATE The vertical location of data on a graph, display monitor, or page layout.

YELLOW The subtractive transparent primary color that should reflect red and green and absorb blue light.

About the Authors

Dr. Richard M. Adams is the research scientist/digital imaging and color reproduction specialist at the Graphic Arts Technical Foundation (GATF); he also currently holds its Apple ColorSync Chair. Adams received an M.S. in printing technology from the Rochester Institute of Technology in 1989, where he specialized in electronic prepress, color scanning, and color measurement. Prior to joining GATF, Adams taught at RIT, California Polytechnic State University, and Illinois State University. Adams has instructed numerous workshops at GATF, and has written a number of articles for *GATFWorld* that have been reprinted as SecondSight technical reports.

Frank J. Romano is the Roger K. Fawcett Distinguished Professor of Graphic Arts at Rochester Institute of Technology, Rochester, New York. Romano teaches electronic prepress and electronic publishing at RIT's School of Printing Management and Sciences. The author of many graphic arts books, including the first book on QuarkXPress, Romano is also the founder of QuarkXPress Users International Association. In addition, he serves as founding editor for the PennWell Graphics Group publications, including *Electronic Publishing*, which he founded in 1977 as *Type World*.

ABOUT GATF

The Graphic Arts Technical Foundation is a nonprofit, scientific, technical, and educational organization dedicated to the advancement of the graphic communications industries worldwide. Its mission is to serve the field as the leading resource for technical information and services through research and education.

For 75 years the Foundation has developed leading edge technologies and practices for printing. GATF's staff of researchers, educators, and technical specialists partner with nearly 14,000 corporate members in over 80 countries to help them maintain their competitive edge by increasing productivity, print quality, process control, and environmental compliance, and by implementing new techniques and technologies. Through conferences, satellite symposia, workshops, consulting, technical support, laboratory services, and publications, GATF strives to advance a global graphic communications community.

The Foundation publishes books on nearly every aspect of the field; learning modules (step-by-step instruction booklets); audiovisuals (CD-ROMs and videotapes); and research and technology reports. It also publishes *GATFWorld*, a bimonthly magazine of technical articles, industry news, and reviews of specific products.

For detailed information about GATF products and services, please visit our website at *http://www.gatf.org* or write to us at 200 Deer Run Road, Sewickley, PA 15143-2600. Phone: 412/741-6860.

GATF*Press*: Selected Titles

- **Understanding Digital Color**
  by Phil Green

- **On-Demand Printing:**
  The Revolution in Digital and Customized Printing
  by Howard Fenton and Frank Romano

- **Glossary of Graphic Communications**
  compiled by Pamela Groff

- **Professional Print Buying**
  edited by Phil Green

- **Handbook of Printing Processes**
  by Deborah Stevenson

- **Flexography Primer**
  by J. Page Crouch

- **Gravure Primer**
  by Cheryl Kasunich

- **Lithography Primer**
  by Daniel G. Wilson

- **On-Demand & Digital Printing Primer**
  by Howard M. Fenton

- **The GATF Encyclopedia of Graphic Communications**
  by Frank Romano and Richard Romano

- **Screen Printing Primer**
  by Samuel Ingram

Colophon

The text of this first edition of *Computer-to-Plate Primer* was created at the Graphic Arts Technical Foundation (GATF) using Microsoft Word, then edited, and called into QuarkXPress 3.31 for Macintosh. The primary fonts used for the interior of the book are New Baskerville and Futura. Illustrations are in TIFF and EPS formats and were created in Adobe Illustrator 8.0 and Adobe Photoshop 5.0.

The cover was printed four-up on a six-color Komori Lithrone 28 sheetfed press and gloss coated. The interior of the book was printed with various size forms on a Heidelberg 40-in. press using 70-lb. Astrolite Monadnock.